LAKE
of the OLD
UNCLES

Also by Gerard Kenney:

Arctic Smoke and Mirrors (1994)
Ships of Wood and Men of Iron (2004)
Dangerous Passage (2006)

LAKE
of the OLD
UNCLES

GERARD KENNEY

DUNDURN PRESS

TORONTO

Copy-editor: Barry Jowett
Proofreader: Allison Hirst
Design: Jennifer Scott
Printer: Marquis

Library and Archives Canada Cataloguing in Publication

Kenney, Gerard I., 1931-
        Lake of the Old Uncles / Gerard Kenney.

ISBN 978-1-55002-802-7

1. Kenney, Gerard L., 1931- 2. Country life--Québec (Province)--Saint-Rémi-d'Amherst Region (Amherst) 3. Natural history--Québec (Province)--Saint-Rémi-d'Amherst Region (Amherst). 4. Saint-Rémi-d'Amherst Region (Amherst, Québec)--Biography. I. Title.

FC2949.S248495Z49 2008   971.4'24204092   C2008-900388-8

1   2   3   4   5   12   11   10   09   08

We acknowledge the support of the **Canada Council for the Arts** and the **Ontario Arts Council** for our publishing program. We also acknowledge the financial support of the **Government of Canada** through the **Book Publishing Industry Development Program** and **The Association for the Export of Canadian Books**, and the **Government of Ontario** through the **Ontario Book Publishers Tax Credit program**, and the **Ontario Media Development Corporation**.

Sketches on pages 45, 53, 76, 81, 116, 148, and 193 © 2008 by Jennifer Foster.
All other illustrations courtesy of the author, except where indicated.

Printed and bound in Canada.
Printed on recycled paper.
www.dundurn.com

Dundurn Press
3 Church Street, Suite 500
Toronto, Ontario, Canada
M5E 1M2

Gazelle Book Services Limited
White Cross Mills
High Town, Lancaster, England
LA1 4XS

Dundurn Press
2250 Military Road
Tonawanda, NY
U.S.A. 14150

TABLE OF CONTENTS

DEDICATION 7

AUTHOR'S ACKNOWLEDGEMENTS 9

A HISTORICAL NOTE ABOUT THE AUTHOR 11

PART I: THE BEGINNING 13

PART II: EARLY DAYS 23

    1. First Fish 25
    2. Friday Pike 27
    3. The Doctor Saves My Bacon 31
    4. Country Medicine 34
    5. Wolf Packs 38
    6. The Pedlar 41
    7. The Train 44
    8. Midnight Mass in the Snow 47

9. First Trout   52

10. The Huge Trout of Tower Lake   58

11. The Porcupine of Lac Croche   62

12. The Green Bottle   66

13. Uncle Lucien's Lesson   72

14. Finding My First Lake   74

PART III: WILD CABINS I HAVE KNOWN   77

1. Philosophy Cabin   80

2. The Cabin on the Jesuit Passage   83

3. The Holmes Lake Cabin   89

4. One Cabin Too Many   92

5. Louie's Tilt   96

PART IV: FARM YEARS   101

1. That Fateful Spring   104

2. Buying a Farm and Settling In   108

3. The First Years on the Farm   115

4. Building the Cabin   130

PART V: LIFE WITH A CABIN   141

1. Our Invisible Friends   144

2. The Canoe   147

3. The Winter Lake   151

4. Time without Boundaries   155

5. The Serene Woods   162

6. The Logbook Speaks   171

PART VI: SHIFTING GEARS   179

PART VII: THE BEST OF FRIENDS   187

DEDICATION

TO DOUGLAS DACRES OF Quebec City, who has been my best friend for some forty-seven years now, sharing with me our common love of nature. Many have been the hikes and canoe outings we have enjoyed together, through sunny times and rainy, and even through a small hurricane, which, one howling night, ripped our floorless tent from over our very heads. To Doug, for being there whenever a partner was needed for a woodsy adventure.

AUTHOR'S ACKNOWLEDGEMENTS

MANY PEOPLE ARE INVOLVED in the successful making of a book, quite a few of them toiling behind the scenes. To all these people I offer my heartfelt thanks for your help. Special thanks go out to my friend Jennifer Foster, whom I met through a serendipitous coincidence, and who offered to grace my book with her beautiful and incomparable sketches.

Many, many thanks to my friend and unofficial editor, Susan, whose numerous frank and incisive suggestions I welcomed and, to a great degree, implemented. Susan was instrumental in soothing down the many rough edges of a manuscript I had thought pretty good until she got a hold of it.

To all who visited the cabin in my absence and left me a note in the logbook – *merci les gars puis les filles!*

And very special thanks go to my lady, Claire, who spent countless hours carefully reading and picking up those bothersome little gremlins that seem to elude almost everybody, especially the author.

A HISTORICAL NOTE
ABOUT THE AUTHOR

IN THE EARLY 1800s, Canadian-born Joseph Papineau was a notary and a political figure in what was then known as Lower Canada — roughly the province of Quebec today. It was the time of seigneurial tenure, a system that had been introduced into New France as a basis of landholding. Large areas of land, called seigneuries, were set aside for the king for granting to lords called seigneurs, and the seigneurs, in turn, had to settle colonists on the land to develop it. One such seigneury, fifteen miles square, the Seigneurie de la Petite Nation, was named after an Algonquin tribe that at one time had lived in the area. In 1803, Joseph Papineau acquired this seigneury, and arrived with nineteen families to settle on it and to develop it. It was located in the area where the villages of Papineauville and Montebello stand today on the shores of the Ottawa River.

One of the nineteen families selected by Papineau to settle on his seigneury was headed by Joseph Thomas dit Tranchemontagne, whose ancestors had arrived in Canada from France in the 1600s. Joseph Thomas dit Tranchemontagne is Gerard Kenney's great-great-great grandfather on his mother's side. The author was born just a few miles

My grandfather Isaïe, extreme right; great-grandfather Norbert, centre; and great-great-grandfather Eustache, next left. All three with the surname Thomas dit Tranchemontagne. Photo circa 1890.

north of the Little Nation Valley in his grandfather's country inn, Hôtel Thomas, at St-Rémi D'Amherst. Many of the events related in this book take place either in the St-Rémi area or in the close-by Little Nation Valley.

Part One

THE BEGINNING

IN THE MOUNTAINS, THE Little Nation River tumbles down in boiling, white-water rapids; in the flatlands, it meanders placidly south through the rolling, green Laurentian fields of Quebec to its rendezvous with the Ottawa River at the French-Canadian town of Plaisance. The town has the distinction of having the longest official name of any municipality in the province of Quebec: Coeur-Très-Pur-de-la-Bien-Heureuse-Vierge-Marie-de-Plaisance — Most Pure Heart of the Very Joyous Virgin Mary of Plaisance. One can understand that the shortened form, Plaisance, is normally, in fact universally, used. Throughout the river's course, from its northern source in Lac Simon to its juncture with the Ottawa River's flow at Plaisance, the surrounding country is called La Vallée de la Petite Nation — the Valley of the Little Nation. The name, it is said, recalls a long-disappeared First Nations settlement of original inhabitants.

There is a small village on the Little Nation River some few dozen kilometres north of its mouth at Plaisance. Another kilometre or two north of the village, a range of forested mountains rises sharply above the valley floor. Not far below the summit of one of the peaks, there dips a depression in the forest floor that cradles a large and deep clear-water pond. Strange place for a pond, near the top of a mountain, but there it is, clear, cool, and spring-fed by underground aquifers located in still-higher mountains some distance away. The local inhabitants call it Lac des Vieux Mon-Oncles. In English, this translates as Lake of the Old Uncles. A drivable dirt track climbs up the mountain peak from the gravelled country road below for some three and a half kilometres to a small, open area where one leaves the car. The last kilometre to the lake is a narrow footpath under a green canopy of rustling sugar-maple leaves.

There is one place, and one place only, around the shore of the lake that is not shallow. At that spot, a steep, rocky cliff falls down the mountainside toward the lake, sharply levelling off just above its surface, creating a sixty-metre, flat plateau of rocky land. Then, just as abruptly, the cliff continues down in its steep plunge into the lake, making that one place ideal for swimming and diving off the rocks. The plateau is just the right size to hold a small log cabin, and indeed there is one there. The lake and the cabin, together with the surrounding three hundred acres of forest, form an oasis of calm, silence, and serenity in the sea of turmoil that is the surrounding world.

I built the cabin, with occasional help when friends visited, largely from the trees of the surrounding forest, and though the physical work of building was started in the spring of 1977 and finished in the summer of 1980, the foundations of the cabin were laid down long ago in the dawn of my life.

In the 1920s, the tiny French-Canadian village of St-Rémi D'Amherst, some thirty miles north of the Valley of the Little Nation, was definitely off the beaten track. All access roads to the village, as well as its streets, were gravel. Sidewalks were of wood. The most imposing building in St-Rémi was the Catholic church. The second-most imposing was Hôtel Thomas, a country inn owned and operated by Isaïe Thomas dit Tranchemontagne and his wife, Amanda. Insignificant as the village might have seemed, it was nevertheless the last stop on the Canadian National Railway line connecting it to Montreal. The reason the CNR line reached as deeply into the Laurentian Hills as it did was the existence of two mines nine miles out of town: one producing kaolin, the other silica. These minerals were shipped in freight cars to Montreal, where they were used in the manufacture of porcelain. There was another small industry in St-Rémi: a sawmill owned by Isaïe's brother, Eustache. The mill was powered by the flowing water of a small creek. It was easy to

Hôtel Thomas, my birthplace, when it was still called Hôtel du Peuple (People's Hotel), circa 1890.

tell that St-Rémi was a sawmill town from the number of men in the village with missing fingers.

One evening in the mid-1920s, the Montreal train brought a stranger looking for a place to board. The trainmen took him in tow and introduced him to Hôtel Thomas, where they themselves boarded. It was fortunate the trainmen spoke English, because the stranger hardly spoke any French, and nobody in St-Rémi spoke English. The stranger was from New York City and worked for a lumber company as a lumber estimator (or "scaler," as they were called because of the long, flexible, wooden rule that was their tool for calculating board-feet of planks). The stranger's company would be buying wood coming out of Eustache's sawmill. His task was to grade the quality of the planks, and measure their quantity in board-feet, before they were loaded into boxcars to be shipped to New York. Eustache's cheque from the lumber company would be based on the lumber scaler's information, which was sent along with the shipments of wood to his New York lumberyard.

Isaïe and Amanda had nine children: six sons and three daughters. Four others had died in infancy before the first lived. The daughters — Albina, Jeanne, and Irene — worked in their parents' inn making up rooms, helping in the kitchen, or serving at tables in the dining room. All three were intrigued by the English-speaking stranger and there began a bit of competition among the three daughters as to who would be waitress in the dining room on any given day. Waitress was the best of the three jobs for making contact with the stranger, who was about the same age as they were. They found out his name was Nason Kenney. The three girls had an intense interest in Nason, and he in them.

At first, communications were necessarily limited. While Nason had a good start in the language, having studied French at university, that in itself doesn't guarantee capability to speak and understand. Nason, in fact, did not possess that capability when he arrived, but everyone in the village marvelled at how quickly he developed fluency in French. He learned to speak French perfectly and without accent. Nason had three good incentives, of course: the Thomas sisters. And besides, there was not much else to do in St-Rémi except to read and speak French, and study the books on the language he had brought with him. His study was helped, of course, by one or more of the daughters.

Nason courted all three girls at first, which did not promote harmony among the trio, but gradually it became evident that the ties developing between him and Jeanne were taking the upper hand. In fact, they became so strong that when Nason was finally recalled to his head office in New York City, he and Jeanne had decided to marry and move to New York as a couple. This was a momentous decision, especially for Jeanne, who spoke only a few words of English and had never been farther away from home and her parents than Montreal, which was only some eighty miles away. There was copious shedding of tears by her mother Amanda, herself, and her two sisters, but love was strong and it prevailed.

The happy couple was married at six o'clock in the morning on April 23, 1928. The marriage took place at such an ungodly hour for a very good reason — the couple had a train to catch. Strictly speaking, the train for Montreal normally left St-Rémi at six in the morning — the very time the marriage was taking place. But on this particular morning, the trainmen, who boarded at Hôtel Thomas and knew Jeanne quite well, discovered that the locomotive had a stubborn technical problem that would take about an hour to fix — coincidentally, of course, making it possible for Nason and Jeanne to get married and still catch the train. Such things could happen in those days. Should one find the right official Canadian National Railway file in the company archives, the documentation would undoubtedly show that an unknown mechanical problem caused the Montreal train to leave St-Rémi an hour late that morning.

The couple set up home in Brooklyn, New York, and while Jeanne went about learning English and making new friends, Nason went to work at the Cross, Austin & Ireland Lumber Company. It wasn't long before Jeanne became pregnant, and in 1929 she presented her husband with a healthy baby boy, whom they named Jacques. Birthing in a hospital amidst a bunch of strangers who could not speak her language — and far from her mother and sisters — had been very difficult for Jeanne, but at least the baby was healthy.

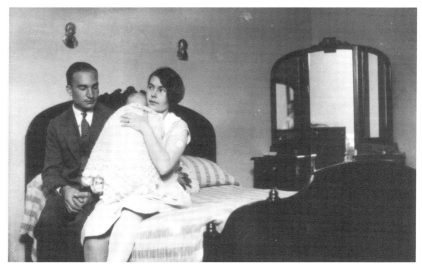

My mother Jeanne and father Nason Kenney in New York City with their first born, Jacques, 1929.

Two years less a few months later, Jeanne again became pregnant and resolved that this time she would not have her baby in a hospital in New York City. She made up her mind to have her second baby in her parents' inn among her people, who of course spoke French: mother, father, sisters, brothers, and her cousin Germaine, who was a nurse and would assist her in giving birth.

One tropical summer evening in early July 1931, Jeanne Thomas warmly embraced her husband, Nason, who had to stay behind because of his work, and bid him goodbye in New York City's Grand Central train station before catching the Delaware & Hudson overnight sleeper to Montreal with her young son, Jacques. Early the next morning, Jeanne was met in the Canadian Pacific Railway's Windsor Station in downtown Montreal by her sister, Albina, who took a taxi with her to Moreau Station in the Maisonneuve quarter of east Montreal. There, Jeanne boarded the CNR train that ran some eighty miles northwest of Montreal, through the prime downhill skiing region of St-Sauveur and Morin Heights, and then clattered through the wild-forested hills all the way on to the end of the line at St-Rémi D'Amherst. At the St-Rémi train station that evening, Jeanne's parents, Amanda and Isaïe, waited impatiently, listening for the distant, mournful whistle of the steam locomotive to echo through the hills to the south of the village as the ever-watchful engineer warned potential motorists on the paralleling dirt road that the railway crossing would not be a healthy place to be for the next few moments. Finally, they heard it, high in the mountains on the far side of Lac Rémi: a long and mournful *whoooo, whoooo, woo, whoooo* — the railway code for a crossing — echoing faintly in the distance.

Fifteen long minutes more and the train finally rounded the end of Lac Rémi, rattling, hissing, and puffing down the final stretch of straight track into town, where it screeched and huffed to a stop with a final, steamy sigh and sat there, catching its breath it seemed, like a huge, exhausted, prehistoric beast. Jeanne's parents lovingly embraced their daughter and grandson Jacques, and showered them with kisses as their daughter climbed down the steps of the railway car with her precious bundle. They quickly hustled mother and son into their car and drove them to their home in the inn, where Jeanne stretched out to rest — tired, but home at last, with Jacques nestled safely in his grandmother's arms.

And so it came to pass that, two weeks later, on July 15, 1931, I was born among my people in room 2 of my grandparents' country inn. In retrospect, it was a fine way to start a life. A few weeks after my birth, Jeanne bid goodbye to her family and, with me and my brother Jacques, boarded the train back to New York where my father, Nason, waited impatiently to greet his family and to meet his new son.

Brooklyn, one of the five boroughs of New York City, was my home for the next fifteen years of life. The year following my birth, my mother began what would become a yearly event. She and her two sons travelled to Canada to spend July and August in St-Rémi with her parents in their country inn. Tragically, in the year I turned two and my brother turned four, he died in a Montreal hospital of acute appendicitis. This was a terrible blow for my parents, but it did not stop my mother from going

My great-grandfather, Norbert Thomas, centre, holding my mother, Jeanne, on his right knee. Back row extreme left are my grandmother, Amanda, and grandfather, Isaïe, holding his daughter, Irene. My grandfather's daughter, Albina, is on the right, holding her cheek on the elderly lady's arm. Photo circa 1907.

back home to Canada every year for the summer months, though with only one son from then on. Almost every year, my father took his two weeks of holidays and joined us in Canada before we all returned to New York together for Labour Day and school.

For fifteen years, I spent the two wonderful vacation months of summer with my mother at her parents' country inn in St-Rémi, as well as one memorable Christmas season. In 1948, when I was sixteen years old, my father died suddenly in New York, after which my mother and I moved back to Canada where I have lived ever since. Those two months every year among my extended family in my early years were the most significant formative periods of my life. It is there that I learned the joys of living in the country, surrounded by nature. Many of those joys revolved around the natural world of forest and lakes, to which I was introduced at a very early age by my grandfather, my mother's six brothers, and other men of the village. Those formative months marked me forever and moulded my spirit in a way that still makes it essential for me to stay in close contact with the world of trees, wild flowers, animals, serenity, and quietude — in other words, the natural world. I was set on the path that, one day, many years later, would lead me to build a log cabin on the shore of an isolated mountain lake in Quebec's Valley of the Little Nation.

Part Two

EARLY DAYS

FIRST FISH

MY GRANDFATHER, Isaïe Thomas dit Tranchemontagne, never treated me as a child. He looked upon me as a person who just had not yet lived the experiences he had, and he shared those experiences with me. He started me off on the path that, years later, led to the cabin on Lake of the Old Uncles. He did that by taking me fishing when I could still barely walk or talk. We were a Catholic family, as was every other family in the village, so Fridays were meatless. Every Friday afternoon, Grandfather Isaïe stepped out the back door of Hôtel Thomas, detoured through the shed for his equipment, and walked across the road with his fishing line and a stocked bait bucket to the rowboat drawn up on the shore of Lac Rémi. He cast off into the weedy waters to troll for the family's supper. But before that, there had been the business of catching minnows for bait, and that is where I came in, in my early days.

On Friday mornings, Grandfather Isaïe walked to the south end of the village, where silvery minnows loved to mark time in the stream, slowly waving their fins in the cool shade under the wooden bridge, just keeping up with the gentle current. He left the inn with an alder branch on his shoulder, a bucket in his hand, slices of bread in his pocket, and me. I was still too young to go in the rowboat with him to catch the big, thrashing pikes in Lac Rémi, but at least I could "help" him catch minnows for bait.

His technique was simplicity itself. He carefully rolled up a small piece of bread into a tiny, doughy, white ball between his thumb and forefinger and gently impaled it on the tip of the hook. Grandpa used hooks with the barb filed off to make it easy to get the minnows off. Now, a little ball of compressed bread does not last long in water before it disintegrates, but then, it didn't have to last very long. As soon as he dropped the bait into the water, the minnows went crazy. They immediately recognized it as something to eat and they furiously thrashed all around it in a miniature feeding frenzy. The advantage of using bread was that it was so soft it didn't impede the hook from penetrating the soft lips of the minnows. I watched in rapt attention as Grandpa pulled in the flip-flopping minnows, carefully unhooking them from the barbless hooks and dropping them into the water-filled bucket.

One day, when I must have been about four, Grandpa read my mind. He asked me in French — that was all he spoke — if I wanted to catch a minnow. "*Ah, oui!*" I nodded excitedly. That was definitely what I most wanted to do. He baited the hook and then curled my hands around the butt end of the alder rod, squeezing them gently. "*Bon,*" he said. "Let's drop the hook in the water." He guided my hands and we slowly lowered the baited hook into the stream. In a second, he pulled my hands sharply up, and there at the end of the line, dangling and dancing, was a silver-sided minnow, which he took gently in his hand, freed from the hook, and dropped into the bucket with the others. "There," he said, looking down at me, "you've caught a minnow." The very next time we got a minnow he carefully removed it from the hook and gently put it in my hands, then covered my hands with his big, gnarled ones, whispering, "Now, hold it, but don't squeeze too hard." Then he slowly released my hands. "Now drop it into the bucket."

I was only a few years old when Grandpa initiated me into the ranks of the village fishermen by teaching me to catch my first minnows. I was impressed. It was a big moment in my young life. This was also the beginning of a close relationship between my grandfather and me, focused largely on the world of fishing.

CHAPTER TWO

FRIDAY PIKE

CATCHING A PIKE in Lac Rémi was pretty well a guaranteed thing. I must have been six or seven when Grandpa first introduced me to the big leagues of fishing when he involved me in catching the family's Friday pike. Oh, how I loved those weekly fishing expeditions. They were a lot more exciting than catching minnows. There was real action here.

We used his Verchères rowboat, which was the best kind of rowboat one could get in those days. These boats were made in the Quebec village of Verchères on the south shore of the mighty St. Lawrence River not far from Montreal. Old craftsmen had been lovingly creating these works of art for decades, passing the skill on from father to son.

I never questioned Grandpa's "rowing" technique. But his technique was a bit unusual, as I realized later on. Grandpa didn't row the boat with the pair of oars that came with it; he used just one oar and sat on the back seat, paddling the boat like a canoe. I sat facing him on the seat that was normally used for rowing.

Grandpa knew exactly how far out from shore the weed beds extended at every point around the lake, and he paddled us along a few feet on the lake side of the beds so that our fishing gear would not get fouled by the weeds. Just before pushing off from shore, he had gathered a few small rocks and thrown them into the boat. Every once in a while he picked up and cast a rock into the weeds to scare any pike out into the open water where our trolling line would be passing by.

His fishing gear was simple. The lure was a gang of four or five bright, reflecting, metal spoons spinning on a steel wire that had a very business-like, three-pronged hook on one end. At the other end it was tied to the fishing line. Bait was the minnows we caught earlier in the day, sometimes accompanied by freshwater clams impaled on the hook, leaving an attractive, watery trail of scent to attract the pike. The heavy line was woven of grey and white cotton that I am sure could easily have held at least two of the biggest, thrashing pike in Lac Rémi at the same time. The line was wound on a flat, oblong piece of cedar with a hand-hole carved in it for carrying, whittled with a pocket knife by Grandpa to receive many turns of line. He unrolled the length he needed and then secured the wooden holder by tying it to the seat I sat on. The other end of the line, the one with the lure and bait on it, he twirled around his head like an Argentine gaucho would his bolo balls, and let fly in a direction away from the boat. I could never help myself from ducking and blinking my eyes when he did that, but not once did he ever misjudge.

After the lure splashed into the water, it was my turn to become involved. While Grandpa started paddling and navigating the boat just the right distance away from the weedy shore, I picked up the plaited line and, under his direction, slowly payed it out until he said, "*assez*," "enough." My job was to hold the line in my hand to detect any fishy vibrations on the other end, and to wait — mostly wait. When a fish did smash into the bait at the far end and set the line to jerking, tugging, vibrating, I bounced up and down with excitement, yelling, "It's a big one!" Grandpa quickly took over the line and pulled it in, hand-over-hand, finally lifting the wildly thrashing pike into the boat. When I became more experienced, he let me play the fish and boat them myself. I felt like I had been promoted. Grandpa knew what he was doing — he was feeding me responsibility as fast as I could take it.

While I held the line firmly wrapped around my hand as he paddled, there were long periods with no action, and if it was sunny and warm, my head tended to nod with drowsiness and I would drift off into a dreamy reverie secure in the knowledge that a biting fish would tug me awake. One day, sharp tugs pulled at my hand as I dozed. Fully awake, I screamed to Grandpa that a huge fish was biting, but Grandpa was doubled over laughing. I quickly caught on. He was the big fish shaking the line. He never tired of these tricks, and I always got caught — more often than the fish did.

Every once in a while, though, Grandpa was not doubled over laughing when I yelled that there was a fish on the end of the line. Those times, I saw him quickly swing into action to firmly set the hook and fight the fish to the boat. To be honest about it, he didn't really play the fish, he just pulled it in firmly. The line was strong enough to hold a small submarine and a pike's mouth is very tough, so there was little danger of tearing the hook out. A pike has only one response to being hooked: it curves its long body in a way that creates maximum drag on the line. The real action only starts once the fish is thrashing in the bottom of the boat. Then the pike starts putting up the desperate fight that would have been more useful to it while still in the water. The show is remarkable and exciting for a youngster, especially when it is taking place at his feet. Pike are big, and the

At fourteen with a good-sized pike from Lac Rémi, caught by myself, 1945.

flopping around they do is impressive, wildly shaking and rattling the lure's string of shiny metal spoons. Grandfather's way of ending the struggle rapidly was to put his jackknife blade through the top of the fish's head and thrust it into the brain. A final tremor and the show was over.

One day, shortly after Grandpa had started letting me pull in the fish and boat them myself, I caught the pike I've never forgotten. When trolling a line behind the boat, every once in a while I pulled it in to check the bait to make sure it was still securely on the hook and not dragging any weeds. On this particular day, I had pulled in almost all the line and was just starting to lift the gang of spoons and hook into the boat when out of the black, watery depths came roaring like a freight train a huge, toothy, gaping maw that clamped itself onto the baited hook just a few inches from my fingers. My instant and violent reaction was to let out a despairing scream of utter panic and heave myself backward into the bottom of the boat, which, unfortunately, pulled the huge, thrashing pike in right on top of me since in my panic I had forgotten to let go of the line. Urgently scrambling out from under the flailing monster and scuttling desperately to the back compartment of the boat, I grabbed Grandpa's legs for protection and looked up at him with terrified eyes the size of saucers. Grandpa was near to falling off his seat, shaking with laughter. After a while, I started laughing a bit, too. What else could I do?

I didn't feel like eating pike for supper that night.

CHAPTER THREE

THE DOCTOR SAVES MY BACON

TWO CENTS WAS a lot of money when I was nine years old in the thirties, and I thought long and hard before accepting Omer St-Pierre's proposal.

"Bet you won't give me two cents to jump off!" he challenged one summer day when we were playing on the roof of Jean-Marie's garage.

Jean-Marie was my uncle, my mother's brother, and his garage was just behind my grandfather's country inn in St-Rémi D'Amherst. Omer was about a year older than I was, and was forever challenging me one way or another. I couldn't let this one go by. I didn't think he'd do it, but I thought about it for a couple of seconds anyway before answering.

"Sure, I'll bet ya two cents ya won't jump off," I bravely challenged back, and sat down on my haunches to wait for him to chicken out.

To my great surprise, Omer carefully approached the edge of the roof, took his measure, and jumped. Quickly, I slid myself over to the edge of the roof to see how he made out.

"Ha, ha! Give me my two cents!" he grinned up at me, obviously unhurt, which I sort of regretted. I was devastated monetarily, but my honour required me to pay up. Reluctantly, I dropped my two cents to him. This was a major loss. In the heat of the moment, I got really brave

— call it stupid — and yelled down at him, "Will you give me my two cents back if I jump, too?"

"Sure," he grinned up at me, "You haven't got the guts to do it!"

There was no way out of it now. I carefully positioned myself on the roof's edge and peered down. The ground appeared much farther away than I wished. I hesitated a few seconds, uncertainty swirling around in my brain. "Nya, nya," mocked Omer up at me. "What a 'fraidy-cat."

Well, that did it. I took my courage in my two hands, as we say in French, mumbled a quick prayer, and jumped. Hitting the ground, my legs folded up, sending my knees shooting up toward the sky. The left one did okay, but the right one, zooming up at a hundred miles an hour, cracked me under the jaw. My head exploded like I had been served a sucker punch uppercut by a heavyweight boxer. I was literally stunned. Shooting stars and excruciating pain flooded my numb brain as I came out of it. As I lay there, Omer hovered over me and dropped something on my chest. "Here's your two cents," he said with regret in his voice. Not regret that I had hurt myself, but regret that he had to give me back my two cents.

After some minutes, my legs regained enough strength to lift me upright. The right knee hadn't suffered, but my jaw sure had. Finally, I was able to walk, and headed straight home to my bedroom to recover. My mother came to see me and asked how I was. I told her that I was a bit tired as I lay there on the bed with the right side of my throbbing face buried in the pillow.

"I'll call you for supper in about half an hour," she said.

Lying there, I felt my jaw. The right side was ballooning out. That worried me, because it was going to be pretty hard to hide, and there was no way I would tell my mother about my two-cent adventure. God only knew what she might do to me.

"Supper's ready!"

I didn't want to go, but what else could I do? Trying to hide my jaw with my hand, I sat down, but my mother saw right through my attempt at camouflage.

"What's wrong with your face?" she questioned.

"I don't know," I lied.

"What do you mean you don't know? Let me see that."

I dropped my hand and displayed my sore jaw with a huge swelling puffing out under the right side.

"*Mon Dieu!* How long have you had that?"

"It started after lunch," I answered truthfully, leaving out the details of why it was there.

"Sit right there," she said. "I'm going to call your grandfather to come and have a look at this."

My grandfather was a kind of folk doctor. He had never actually studied medicine, but he seemed to have a folk remedy for just about every sickness St-Rémi could produce. And so, it was natural that he was the first person my mother went to.

But this case had even Grandpa stumped. He came over from his inn, examined my swollen jaw, and decided that my mother had better take me to see the nearest doctor, who was in St-Jovite, some fifteen miles away. Uncle Jean-Marie got his car ready. My mother and I got in and, as we backed out of the garage, I glanced out through the side window and saw the marks in the sand where I had landed an hour or so before. I hoped no one else would notice them.

The doctor carefully examined the swollen side of my jaw, muttered a few "hmms," then examined the unswollen left side with a few more "hmms," and finally straightened up to announce, "Well, this is a most remarkable case. There's a lot of mumps going around right now, and that's what this looks like, but it's the first time I've ever seen a case of unilateral mumps."

"What are unilateral mumps?" asked my mother.

"Mumps on only one side," answered the doctor. "This is the first time I have ever come across such a case. Just keep him in bed for a few days and feed him a lot of liquids. I'm sure he'll be okay, but call me if any complications develop."

Whew! I breathed a low sigh of relief. The good doctor had unwittingly saved my bacon. Being in bed for a couple of days was nothing, next to what my mother would have done to me had she found out what really happened. Besides, being in bed with my sore, throbbing jaw was exactly where I wanted to be right then, with my two cents safely wrapped in a handkerchief and deep in my pocket.

My poor mother went to her grave many years later believing her wonderful son had had unilateral mumps that summer when he was young. She never knew how stupid he had really been for two cents, and I surely would never have enlightened her.

CHAPTER FOUR
COUNTRY MEDICINE

I REALLY LOVED my grandfather, not just because he took me fishing, but because he was a rock of security for a young grandson. When he was around, nothing bad could happen. Just being around him, I picked up other valuable life skills. His experience rubbed off on me.

As I have said, besides fishing, Grandpa Isaïe was also noted in the area as a fine folk doctor — another skill that impressed me. When Grandpa announced to the family one day that he was going to have to resort to *la ventouse* to treat his son Gilles, we all knew that my uncle was pretty sick. *La ventouse* was the ultimate weapon in Grandfather's arsenal of Quebec folk medicine.

Since he was the village innkeeper, it was natural for him to hold most of his medical consultations right there in the barroom of Hôtel Thomas. He was essentially a non-drinker himself, so it was ironic not only that he saw to the needs of the thirsty as an innkeeper, but also that many of his remedies for internal disorders called for alcohol. To my grandfather's way of thinking, I didn't have enough meat on my bones when I was young. He instructed my mother to beef me up with brandy eggnogs for breakfast. I don't know how much the eggnogs helped improve my health, but I do know that for once I was in full agreement with Grandpa's prescription. The eggnogs were delicious.

Rum was another powerful medicine in Grandpa's bag of cures. Anything resembling a bad cold or grippe was promptly attacked with a barrage of hot *ponces* mixed of rum, lemon, honey, and spices dissolved in boiling water. Right after drinking the steaming *ponce*, the patient took to his bed and was covered over with layers of thick blankets. The combination of rum, hot water, spices, and blankets induced a heavy sweat that was followed by a deep sleep. It was not at all unusual for the patient to awaken refreshed and feverless after a few treatments, although a touch on the weak side.

Grandfather's powerful medicines were not based only on alcohol. Ménard's Liniment was another of his favourites. He used it for all those aches and pains that normally respond to the powerful, penetrating effect of liniment, such as sprains, strains, charley horses, etc. But to limit its application to such plebeian ailments would have been to deny the full power of Ménard's — in Grandpa's eyes, anyway. He had such a reverent awe for the curative powers of this liniment that he relied on it for a much wider range of applications than most users. I still have a very vivid memory of that early winter evening when the patriarch, bottle of Ménard's liniment in hand, followed Grandma Amanda up the stairs to their bedroom. His wife had been complaining lately that her haemorrhoids were distressing her. The bedroom door clicked shut behind the elderly couple and an uneasy silence settled upon the kitchen below, where we waited in suspense — but not for long. A howling, blood-curdling screech of pain penetrated every square inch of the country inn and some distance beyond. A few moments passed, then Grandpa stumbled a bit unsteadily down the stairs, bottle of Ménard's still in hand, visibly shaken by the extreme effect of his favourite medicine. Grandma never again complained of her ailment and Grandpa pointed to this fact as irrefutable proof of the effectiveness of his cure.

But *la ventouse* was unquestionably Grandpa's most dramatic cure, reserved for the gravest of cases. So when I heard that Uncle Gilles was to get the treatment, I arranged to be there next to his bed. A kerosene lamp pushed a flickering sphere of yellow light into the bedroom like a large balloon pressing out against the surrounding gloom. Prostrate on the bed lay Uncle Gilles, stripped to the waist, body flushed with fever, racked by paroxysms of coughing. The circle of anxious attendants included my mother (Uncle Gilles' sister), Grandpa, Grandma, and me — an unnecessary but curious eleven-year-old observer. Uncle Gilles' malaise had lasted for a week now, and instead of improving, it had resolved itself into an ugly chest cough. The nearest doctor lived in Huberdeau, a long ways away by horse and sleigh. All possible home remedies had to be exhausted before such a trip could be imposed on good Doctor Emery. Hot *ponces* had been followed by mustard plasters amplified by vigil lamps burning to the attention of St. Jude, patron saint of hopeless cases. Uncle Gilles' case was not hopeless yet, but it was felt that Jude might perhaps cross jurisdictional boundaries and help out anyway. None of these efforts had succeeded. The time had clearly come to call upon the potency of *la ventouse*.

Beer glasses were fetched from the bar, together with the previous day's copy of the newspaper, *La Presse*, and some matches. Thin strips of newspaper were cut from *La Presse*, each about three-quarters of an inch wide and three inches long. The equipment was ready.

Grandpa picked up one of the paper strips and carefully folded a one-inch tab on the end of it so that it looked like the capital letter "L." He applied his tongue to the tab, daubing it with saliva, and pressed it to the skin of Uncle Gilles' back. The strip stood up like a little mast, two inches vertically, with a one-inch horizontal tab sticking to the skin by the power of saliva. Grandpa struck a match and lit the end of the little paper mast. Once Grandma saw that the paper was burning well, she clapped an inverted beer glass over it. The paper burned down toward the skin, but then went out quite suddenly before reaching it as the oxygen in the glass gave out. At the same time, the skin of Uncle Gilles' back was sucked up into the glass about three-quarters of an inch by the force of the powerful vacuum created when the oxygen was consumed. The suction of *la ventouse* was reputed to draw the disease-causing element out through the skin. Another five of the sucking *ventouses* were applied and left in place before Uncle Gilles' treatment could be said to have begun. For the next half hour, the four of us hovered anxiously over the sickbed as the *ventouses* exerted their magic force. The gloomy minutes were punctuated by the tinkling of the glasses as Uncle Gilles' coughing fits caused two of the glasses that were too close to each other to clink together. After thirty minutes of treatment, the patient was judged to have endured enough of *la ventouse*'s curative powers. Grandma started pulling off the glasses, each one popping as it released its vacuum. Circles of angry red welts marked the areas where the disease had left the body. The patient coughed a sigh of relief. I was relieved, too.

I am glad to say that Uncle Gilles survived his illness as well as its treatment. Whether it was due to the *ponces*, the mustard plasters, St-Jude, *la ventouse*, or just plain time is still unresolved in my mind, but one thing is certain: in the minds of Uncle Gilles, Grandpa, and Grandma, there was no doubt. It was *la ventouse* — with perhaps a bit of catalytic stimulation from St-Jude.

CHAPTER FIVE

WOLF PACKS

AS A YOUNG BOY, I always felt welcome in my grandfather's barroom, helping him out. It was probably against some law for me to be carrying bottles of beer to his patrons at my age and the authorities would not have been amused, but there were never any authorities in the village, anyway. They just weren't needed there. Drinking beer in a country inn in Quebec was not a violent sport in those days — most of the time anyway.

Whenever I needed to talk to someone about important questions to do with fishing, hunting, or the woods, I could always count on Grandpa to hear me out. Sometimes the wise old men in the barroom listening in would offer their advice. Pungent, blue smoke curled up from the home-grown tobacco smouldering in their pipes while they sat sipping beer, and occasionally tucking a few strands of tobacco into their mouths, chewing and aiming brownish streams of juice at the spittoons on the floor. So, on the afternoon I got chased out of the forest by wolves, I ran back to the village — and Grandpa — as fast as I could on fear-inspired legs. With beating heart and breathless lungs, I burst into the barroom of Hôtel Thomas to spill out the story of my scary encounter.

My uncles had begun taking me out on the forest trail that started at the base of the mountains on the outskirts of St-Rémi and wound its way to the nearest trout lake in the forest not far from the village. Premier Lac — First Lake — was its unimaginative name. We fished, but hardly ever caught much there because the lake was too close to town and every boy in the village dipped his line in First Lake. On a warm day in spring, I got the urge to go to the lake by myself, not so much to fish, but just to taste the thrill of being on my own in the woods, which I had yet to experience alone. The footpath was well-worn and there was really little danger of my getting lost. I told Grandpa what I wanted to do and he heartily agreed. He gave me a few words of advice about using the sun's position to guide me so as not to get turned around, and off I trotted right after lunch on my adventure.

The path led through some cow pastures back of the village and then into the lightly wooded hills before the real forest took hold. A cow and a horse had died back there some years past and I passed their bleached skulls still lying on the ground. There was something unsettling about their hollow eye sockets and grinning teeth. I had seen them before with my uncles, but this time I was alone. They spooked me, and the self confidence in what I was doing went down a notch. After looking around for a moment a bit apprehensively, I carried on into the forest.

It was not long before I reached the shore of the lake. I was feeling a bit proud of myself over this accomplishment, but then I heard something that made the hair bristle on the back of my neck. Across the lake from where I stood spread the wide flank of a high mountain. From that flank, the yapping of a pack of wild animals came echoing across the lake to my ears. Because of the echoes, it was hard to tell exactly where the yapping was coming from. It seemed to be from the forest on the right-hand extremity of that flank, but it was moving, very quickly it seemed, across the flank from right to left and dying off in the distance. I was petrified. Before I could do anything, another pack of the same kind of animal started calling, again in the right-hand corner of the mountain flank, and again they were moving swiftly from right to left. I was frightened by how fast they could lope from one side of the mountain to the other. I was sure they were wolves, probably coming around the end of the lake on my left to get at me. I wasted no time.

I hightailed it back down the trail as fast as I could. The forest petered out into the lightly wooded lower slope and I flew past the grisly, grinning skulls of the cow and horse, the sight of which boosted me up to top speed, before finally ending up in the grassy cow pastures below. Only then did I dare to slow down some. It crossed my mind that the original owners of those skulls had probably been eaten by wolves some years ago. Lord, I was glad to see the houses of the village again. I didn't think wolves came out of the forest into the open pastures, so I slowed down to a fast walk to catch my breath, but I didn't stop ... not until I got to the safety of Hôtel Thomas.

Grandpa was behind the bar drying glasses with a cloth when I rushed in, my chest heaving for want of air. "Whoa," he said, "what's going on here? I thought you were gone to First Lake."

"I was," I answered hoarsely. "I got all the way to the lake, but when I got there I was chased out of the woods by two packs of wolves."

Grandpa calmly put down his dish towel and said, "Wolves, eh? Let's tell the boys about this." So, I breathlessly repeated my story for the two old men sitting in a haze of blue at a round table in the barroom, enjoying glasses of beer and chewing. Just as my grandfather had, they took my news very calmly. "Wolves, eh?" asked one, turning his head to the side where the spittoon was and aiming a stream of brown at it. "What did they sound like?" inquired the other.

I tried making sounds like the wolves I had heard as best I could, which wasn't a very good imitation. "Hmmm," they both mused as the smoke curled up from their pipes. Suddenly, I saw Grandpa cock his head, listening attentively for a moment. Then he beckoned "Come with me," and led me to the door of the inn opening to the outside. "Was it like that?" I looked up for a long minute, and then, as a flock of Canada Geese flew overhead, honking away, just like the "wolves" at First Lake, I slowly cast my eyes to the floor, admitting very sheepishly, "Yes, just like that." My eyes stuck to the floor with embarrassment. Grandpa closed the door and we both returned to sit down with his two patrons at the round table.

"You see," said Grandpa, "the flank of the mountain echoed the honks of the geese as they flew over and made it sound like they were running through the forest. An easy mistake to make."

"Hmmm," agreed the two old men, nodding their heads and puffing smoke.

"My son," said Grandpa, "you learned something about the forest today. That's good."

And that was the last I heard of it.

CHAPTER SIX

THE PEDLAR

ANOTHER YEAR, I LEARNED a different kind of lesson in Grandpa's barroom, but I didn't understand it until several years later.

The cry went up. "*Le noir est arrivé, le noir est arrivé!*" — "The black man is here." And indeed he was.

Every year in late August, he came shuffling down the dirt road leading into St-Rémi. Draped on his arm was a morning coat. His shirt was white and soaked with sweat. A black bow tie wilted at his neck. His head was shaded by a black top hat, and grey spats protected his shoes. The man carried a large, black, leather satchel, shifting it from one hand to the other to relieve the obvious heaviness of it. He had a powerful build, accentuated by a great, barrel chest. As he approached the village, the man stopped and put on his morning coat, which complemented his grey, striped pants. The air about him was elegant, if perhaps a bit dusty, threadbare, and travel-worn. The tired shuffle changed to a jaunty stride as he neared the first houses on the outskirts of St-Rémi. He threw back his head and wore a huge smile when he encountered his first potential customers, for the man was an itinerant pedlar.

I was used to seeing black people, since I lived in Brooklyn during the school months, but for my summer friends in St-Rémi in the early forties, a black man in town was a very rare sight. For most of the kids, the pedlar was the only black person they had ever seen in the flesh. He resembled a modern-day Pied Piper as the children of St-Rémi followed him through the dusty dirt streets of the village, dancing and shouting with excitement.

The clamour summoned the village women to their front doors. They knew the pedlar from years past and remembered that he had many useful things to sell. One woman bought buttons that she needed, another some thread and needles. There were combs, mirrors, little sacred pictures of Jesus, Mary, and Joseph, Jew's harps, straight pins, safety pins, hairpins — all kinds of things. On the inside of his satchel, in the corner at one end, was a fair-sized compartment held shut by two metal snaps. This pocket, the pedlar didn't open for the village women. But all his other treasures they could see — and buy.

The procession danced its way through the village, growing longer and noisier as the latecomers jostled in. Just about in the middle of the village, the pedlar made a special stop. Here he went inside Hôtel Thomas. All the children waited outside — all except me. I just followed him in. After all, this was where I lived in the summertime.

The barroom of the inn was a meeting place for the village's lumberjacks, who had nothing better to do in the long, hot days of summer than spend their hard-earned winter's wages drinking beer and reliving their adventures of the past winter in the lumber shanties. In those days, lumberjacking was a trade practised only in winter. Summer was a fallow season for these iron-muscled men.

I was on the pedlar's heels as he entered the barroom to be greeted by the hoots and hollers of the lumberjacks when they recognized their old friend. Nobody paid much attention to me. They were used to seeing me in the barroom helping out my grandfather. The pedlar went up to the bar and was greeted by Grandpa like a long-lost friend. A cold beer was set down in front of him to counter the effects of the hot summer sun. After a while, Grandpa gave the pedlar another beer. Refreshed, the man was ready for business.

It was there in the barroom that the pedlar opened his satchel and finally unsnapped the special compartment in the corner and took out the treasures that none of the women had set eyes on. The lumberjacks were obviously interested, and whatever the items were, many were bought. They came in little silver-and-brown tins about the size and shape of an aspirin tin. I could make out the word "SILVER" in big letters on the covers, but that was all. The lumberjacks laughed and joked about the dance the following Saturday, and the girls they would meet. It was then that my mother saw me through the barroom door. Women weren't allowed in the barroom then, but that didn't prevent her from rushing over to me, grabbing me by the arm, and dragging me away. She pushed me out the door of the inn to join my friends, who were waiting impatiently on the front steps for the pedlar to reappear.

A great cry went up as the black man finally came out, and the procession continued down the main street to the end of the village, with a comb sold here, some needles there, hairpins here, a mirror there, but to the women, no little tins marked "SILVER."

Finally, the pedlar reached the end of the village, set down his satchel, took off his hat and coat, and wiped his brow with a large, rumpled, white handkerchief. He waved to all us kids and shuffled on down the road to Lac des Plages, the next village, thirteen kilometres away.

It was several years before I finally understood the lumberjacks' appreciation for the visit of the black pedlar. For this was Catholic Quebec in the forties, and little tins marked "SILVER" were not sold in St-Rémi.

CHAPTER SEVEN
THE TRAIN

EVERY DAY AFTER SUPPER, when the sun had set and the refreshing coolness of the quiet summer evenings came on, the men of the village gravitated toward the front porch of Hôtel Thomas, gathering in anticipation of an event that would complete their day. They had left their grimy work clothes at home, having exchanged them for cleaner ones to go with their well-scrubbed hands and faces and neatly combed back hair. They had replaced their honest daytime perfume of spruce and fir with strong cologne from a bottle. Their talk was desultory, just filling in time until they heard what they had come to hear. Across the road from the inn, spreading out both to the left and right, the sparkling surface of Lac Rémi danced with the light of the setting sun on clear evenings. From the darkening mountains across the lake, far off to the right, miles away yet, came the haunting and lonely cry of a rushing locomotive signalling that it was approaching a crossing. The group of men arose as one, and I with them, to walk leisurely to the station a few hundred metres away. Then, several minutes later, out of a distant valley to the right of Lac Rémi, came the narrow, yellow beam of the loco's headlight, piercing the gathering dusk, accompanied by the

faraway chugging of the engine and the faint sound of the train's wheels clattering on the steel rails.

This was the same train my parents had taken, in the opposite direction toward Montreal, on their way to New York City the morning of their wedding in the St-Rémi church many years before. In the evening, the train arriving at St-Rémi had to run the length of the far side of the lake from right to left and do a looping horseshoe turn around the end before finally heading toward the village and the station. By the time we walked from the inn to the station, the train would just be coming in, rattling and puffing and screeching to a stop in a hissing cloud of steam. The resting locomotive sat there panting, as if to catch its breath, steam rising from its body as from a racehorse after a long, hard run.

It was not as if we were there to meet passengers getting off the train — there were usually only a half a dozen or so. They were most often men who had business with the Kasil mine fifteen kilometres away and needed to get something to eat and spend the night at Hôtel Thomas. There were two good reasons why the men of the village met the train in the evening:

one was that it was something to do, and the other, an equally important one, was that the train carried mail.

As soon as the train arrived, the mailbags were tossed out of the baggage car and carried over to Amédé Rousseau's butcher shop, a short distance away from the station. Madame Rousseau was the postmistress, and now she had work to do in a side room — off the butcher shop proper — that served as the post office. She had to sort out the mail and the newspapers. Almost everyone read *La Presse*. The village men sauntered over to the post office, knowing that there was no need to hurry because it took Madame Rousseau at least ten to fifteen minutes to complete her sorting. Gradually, the post-office room filled up, mostly with men and occasionally a woman or two. It was the man's job to get the mail. Those who didn't fit in overflowed out the door. An expectant hush fell over those waiting, and finally Madame Rousseau began calling out names: "Hector Thomas!" "René St-Louis!" "Joseph Lavigne!" "Isaïe Thomas!"— that was my grandfather! Like the others, I reached over those in front and got my grandfather's newspaper and mail from the hands of Madame Rousseau and wriggled my way back through the crowd to the outside, heading home to the inn.

When the men got their mail and newspaper, they also walked back to their homes to spend the evening reading *La Presse* — and if they were lucky, their mail — by the feeble light of kerosene lamps. Village life was over for the day.

CHAPTER EIGHT
MIDNIGHT MASS IN THE SNOW

JEANNE THOMAS DIT TRANCHEMONTAGNE was a religious woman, a French-Canadian Catholic woman, who never lost her language nor her culture, despite twenty-some-odd years living in Brooklyn with her agnostic husband, my father, Nason. A contributing factor to Jeanne's remaining a solid French Canadian was my father's deep interest in the French culture and his remarkable capacity for learning the language, eventually speaking it without a trace of accent, and quite as well as my mother. Our family language when we were together was French. My school language was English. My father spoke English with me, and my mother spoke French. This scheme pretty well guaranteed that I would be bilingual, although that was not a goal — it just happened. My parents came to a religious compromise. Nason stuck to his deeply ingrained agnosticism and Jeanne kept the Catholic faith. As far as I was concerned, they agreed that I was to follow my mother's religion until I made up my own mind. Sunday Mass was a compulsory activity for me.

One thing Jeanne sorely missed every year in New York was Midnight Mass at Christmas with her parents and siblings. There were Midnight Masses in New York, of course, but they didn't have the same meaning for her that Midnight Mass in St-Rémi D'Amherst had. She never attended Midnight Mass in New York, where she would have been surrounded by a crush of people she didn't know. At Christmastime, with sadness in her voice, my mother would tell me how much she missed the beauty of Midnight Mass in her country parish. She tried to explain to me why it was so beautiful to go to Midnight Mass in St-Rémi, but words alone could not possibly explain her feelings to me. I just could not understand what could be so beautiful in a mass, which, to be frank, I found quite boring, and I imagined was even more so if it took place in the middle of the night.

My mother had never taken out American citizenship since moving to New York, and in the war year of 1942 my father became concerned that if she left the country for her annual summer visit back home to Canada with me, we might not be allowed back into the U.S. Who knew what could happen in wartime? She had started the process of becoming American, but it would be a few months yet before her citizenship would come through and she could feel free to travel home to St-Rémi. Meanwhile, she cancelled our summer trip, but with the hope that if her citizenship certificate came through in time, she and I would make our trip to St-Rémi at Christmastime that year, which is exactly what happened. And that is how I got to attend Midnight Mass in the snows of Laurentian Quebec that winter. My mother and I took the train from New York and arrived in St-Rémi a few days before the 25th of December.

In the days preceding Christmas, my uncles took me under their wing. Uncle Lucien took me to his trapping grounds and showed me how to snare snowshoe hares with nooses of fine brass wire placed in the runways in the snow used by the hares. These animals were a staple country food and could be found hanging frozen in the back sheds of all the village houses. Lucien also trapped muskrats for their skins, and if an occasional mink got caught, that was even better. Uncle Gérard hitched up my grandfather's mare to the cutter and took me for long rides along the roads, which were not cleared of snow in those days. Cars were all put away in barns for the winter and horses were king. I was intrigued by the way the animals were hitched up to a one-horse sleigh. They were hitched to the right of centre, just enough for their hooves to step in the track worn by the right runner of the cutter. This lopsided arrangement made it easier for sleighs to meet on the road, and it was also easier for the horses because they were trotting in the beaten right-hand rut rather than the deep snow of the centre. Slipping along the pure-white snow was pretty silent. The horses' hooves made very little noise as they thrust against the yielding snow, and the runners' faint swish was effectively muffled by the fluffy powder. The only real sound was the beautiful music of the jingle bells that adorned the horses' winter harnesses.

Christmas Eve arrived and there was a great bustle of the womenfolk in my grandparents' Hôtel Thomas where we stayed. They were cooking up venison, chickens, meat pies, fruit pies, and preparing all else that a *réveillon* calls for. The *réveillon* is the traditional French-Canadian Christmas meal that is eaten right after Midnight Mass — a tradition that persists to this day. While all this was going on, we younger folk — I was eleven years old — were told to lie down upstairs and get some sleep and they would awaken us in time for the mass. It was an effective way of getting us out of the way while everything was prepared for the all-important *réveillon*.

Sleeping youngsters don't take easily to being shaken awake just before midnight. We moved like zombies as our parents bundled us up in layers and layers of warm clothes for the sleigh ride to church through the deep, black cold of a middle-of-the-night Laurentian winter. The men lifted us into the family-sized sleigh and buried us under thick buffalo robes that had been warmed up next to the kitchen stove. There was no moon that night, but the light of thousands of stars that twinkled in the black vault overhead was reflected by the sparkling blanket of white, and that reflected starlight was enough to light the way. At the church, sleighs were arriving from all directions in a jingle-bell symphony of cheery Christmas music. Steaming horses were tied up outside and covered up with thick blankets thrown over their backs to ward off the deep cold while they waited patiently for their masters.

Curé Allard, our parish priest, had been busy in his own way, stoking up the huge wood-burning furnace down in the basement of the church to warm up his temple of prayer to a warmer state than on any other winter night of the year. Electricity was still unknown in St-Rémi in 1942, so hundreds of burning candles and strategically placed lanterns lit up the church. For a reason that is still not clear to me, there are three Midnight Masses at Christmas: a high mass, and two low masses all following one another, any one of which would suffice to fulfill the Christmas-duty requirements of parishioners. But it was the first one, the high mass, that everyone really went to church for. Some of the more religious stayed for all three, but we were not part of that group. One mass — high mass — was good enough for us. After all, *réveillon* was waiting for us.

In French, the term for celebrating a high mass is *chanter la messe* — "to sing the Mass" — and sing it they did. The priest did not simply say a high mass; he literally sang it, and he was not alone. I am still amazed at the musical talent that lay hidden in a small village like St-Rémi, and no doubt in all other small French-Canadian villages throughout Quebec. The counterpoint to the priest's singing was a thundering chorus of rich Gregorian-chanting male voices alternating with a pure, high-pitched, angelic feminine chorus. The singing was accompanied by the powerful strains of a real, furiously pumped pipe-organ in the loft, whose notes filled the church to the very top of its high-vaulted ceiling curving over our heads. The church fairly trembled with music and emotion. I was beginning to understand my mother's longing to attend Midnight Mass at Christmas in her home village, surrounded by her own people.

After the mass, we all filed out of the church and gathered on the steps, where there was much kissing and handshaking as we warmly exchanged Christmas wishes with our fellow parishioners. By then, there was a herd of impatient, and cold, snorting horses pawing the snow outside the church. We were bundled back into the sleigh and the horse quickly glided us home to the warmth of the hotel where *réveillon* awaited us.

The term *réveillon* comes from the same root as *réveiller*, which means "to wake up." Well, the *réveillon* does that, all right. Even though it may be two o'clock in the morning, all thought of sleep is banished, for *réveillon* is a major event.

Before the eating, there had to be the toasting, of course — a toast to everyone's health, prosperity, and love, and once again for good measure. Then came the food and more wine, and plenty of it. My favourite dish at Christmas was, and still is, tourtière, which is *de rigueur* for all French-Canadian families at that time of the year. Tourtière is a meat pie that is a throwback, it is said, to times when passenger pigeons darkened the skies of North America. The French word for that bird is *tourte*. Regrettably, there are no more passenger pigeons, so today beef and pork are used instead when making tourtière, but the name remains. Every Québécois woman had her own recipe for the delicacy, each slightly different from the others, so there was an infinity of tourtières to be tasted in a lifetime.

When everybody's belly was sufficiently rounded, the entertainment started. Since there was no television, but only a few hand-wound, scratchy Victrolas, and very little radio in those days, entertainment was do-it-yourself. The lack of canned music and singing allowed natural talents to bloom. There were always fiddlers, accordion, guitar, and piano players, storytellers, step-dancers, and songbirds, all from St-Rémi. Singing involved everyone, thanks to *les chansons à repondre,* which, loosely translated, means "songs one answers to." Everyone participates in these songs, which are easy to remember because the participants repeat lines that are sung just a few seconds before. When the entertainment starts to die down, dawn is not far off and sleepiness begins to show in everyone's eyes as the crowd thins out.

Toys? Oh yes, there were a few toys for the youngsters, but that was not considered a very important part of Christmas, except by us kids,

The following year, when Christmas rolled around once more, my parents and I stayed in New York as was usual at that time of the year. I finally understood and shared my mother's yearning for spending Christmas among her people — my people — in the crisp and frosty Quebec countryside.

CHAPTER NINE

FIRST TROUT

God bless all kind uncles who take small boys fishing.
— from *Brown Waters* by W.H. Blake

IT WAS MY GRANDFATHER who first aroused my curiosity about fishing, but it was my young friend Bernard who introduced me to one particular aspect of the sport that eventually became the only kind of angling for me: catching *Salvelinus fontinalis* — speckled trout.

I had already caught lots of minnows and pike with my grandfather for our Friday suppers, but had yet to have a speckled trout on the end of my line. One summer day, my young friend Bernard took me fishing in a stream he knew that meandered through a farmer's field on the outskirts of St-Rémi. We shouldered our alder-branch rods with balls of black fishing line wrapped around the ends and tramped across the field scaring up clouds of whirring grasshoppers with each footstep. Bait was not a problem.

The brook was narrow, with overhanging banks shading mysterious black pools in the languidly flowing water. We each skewered a squirming 'hopper on our hooks. All us kids knew that grasshoppers oozed molasses

when they were hooked, but none of us had ever tasted the dark brown liquid to see if it really was molasses. We just knew it was.

I dropped my hook into a dark pool under the near bank of the stream. There was an immediate swirl of the water and my rod was sharply wrenched downward, then jerked to one side, and to the other. I just as sharply pulled up and a thrashing fish flew over my head to flop around on the grass behind me.

"Take it in your hand," urged Bernard.

I had never in my life seen such a beautiful fish. Uncle Lucien often brought trout home, but they were stiff and faded in colour by the time I saw them. This one was alive and squirming, with sparkling red rubies in cold, steel-blue settings lining its sides.

"Feel its nerves," instructed Bernard, meaning its muscles. "They're much stronger than a minnow's."

He was right. The trout *was* much stronger than a minnow. I could feel its cold muscles straining desperately. I could feel them straining with a strength no minnow ever had. From that day on, speckled trout have been the only kind of fish for me. They say bass fight harder and that doré — or walleye or pickerel, depending on where you are from — are supposed to taste better, but only a speckled trout on the end of my line can make my heart beat faster.

What Bernard awakened in me on that day, my mother's brothers intensified. Trout fishing was in their blood.

Not far from St-Rémi, the road to Montreal passed near the trout hatchery at St-Faustin. It was not too hard to convince my uncles to take the detour to the hatchery on our car trips to Montreal. The fish were held outdoors in concrete, water-filled basins. Each basin teemed with vigorous fish of the same age. We bought small bags of dried shrimp and scattered them into the artificial ponds. The water boiled with leaping fish, the young ones leaping at anything. We had only to spit in the water to drive them wild. The older and bigger trout in the larger basins displayed a calmness and wariness that came with age and maturity. They were much harder to entice than the carefree small fry.

Large glass aquariums let us get eye to eye with five- and six-pound monsters. Sometimes I would withdraw into a sort of reverie and imagine I had one of those monsters on my line. At times, I even noticed my uncles with faraway looks in their eyes when they stared into the glass aquariums.

One of the aquariums held blind trout. It was at the hatchery that I first learned trout have a chameleon-like characteristic. They adjust their body colouration to match their surroundings as they perceive them through their eyes. The aquarium filled with blind trout held fish that were almost completely black, since that was the only colour they "saw."

A few years later I ran into the other end of the scale. About four miles from St-Rémi, there was a railway station called Kasil. The name was made up from a combination of "*ka*olin" and "si*lica*." There was no real town there, only two mines, one producing kaolin, or China clay, and the other pure white silica sand. The mines' output was shipped to Montreal for making fine porcelain.

Tons of pure-white tailings from the mines were dumped into a large lake near the pits and shafts, and turned the water an opaque, milky colour. You couldn't see more than a couple of inches through it. I never fished that lake, but I did fish the stream that ran out of it and tumbled down the mountainside to the valley below. I once caught speckled trout that lived in that milky-white stream, but they were hardly worthy of the name. They were almost as milky-white as the water in the stream with just the faintest colourless speckles dimly marking their sides. Their flesh was white, too. I never bothered to fish that stream again. I didn't eat the fish either. It just didn't seem healthy.

Back in the forties, country people fished to eat, and not too many "sports" from the city had found their way out to St-Rémi with their fancy equipment. There were lots of fish and no one paid much attention to the game laws. People only took a few for the table as a treat once in a while. The only law was "don't get caught."

Fishing through the ice for speckled trout in winter is not legal in Quebec, nor was it sixty years ago. Trout are vulnerable when the ice is on the lakes. The fish are over their spawning grounds of clean, yellow-coloured sand then, and will bite at anything on a hook lowered down through the ice. It's not that they are hungry, my uncles told me. They just want to keep their spawning beds clear of debris. But the country people back then had a taste for trout as much in winter as during the rest of the year, and besides, keeping two steps ahead of the game warden was all part of the fun, so we caught a few speckleds through the ice the year I spent Christmas in St-Rémi.

My uncles knew where the spawning beds were in all the lakes in the hills around St-Rémi. The beds were always in quiet bays with sandy bottoms and three or four feet of water in them. The sand was clean because it had been cleared of all debris by the spawning fish. We chopped holes with an axe through the foot or so of ice. The holes were shaped like a large eye, pointed at both ends and opening up in the middle. It was easier to chop them in that shape. We didn't need a fishing rod, just a handheld piece of line with a hook and sinker on the end. The hook was decorated with a piece of beef or bacon, or whatever else was on hand — it didn't much matter. We slowly lowered our hooks through the holes and jigged them gently up and down a couple of inches above the sand while stretched out on our stomachs in the snow, peering down the hole. We could see the trout clearly. They looked bigger than they really were. Water magnifies things.

A trout slowly swam over to my dangling bait to take it into its mouth and deposit it somewhere else to keep the spawning bed clean. A sharp jerk and the fish was hooked. I pulled the line up quickly, hand-over-hand, and the trout was soon flopping on the snow ... only it didn't flop around the same as in the summertime. It flopped more slowly and in sort of a spastic way, as if its body were stiff. I guess it must have been, since the water was just about at freezing temperature.

After a while, no more fish came to our baits, so we chopped other holes a little further away. Flopping down on my stomach again I peered through the hole and saw more speckleds hovering over this new section of the spawning bed. Now and then a female worked up a little speed, turned over on her side, her body shuddering and convulsing six or seven times in a row to release her eggs over the nest. Then a male followed — they were distinctly different from the females: head and jaw were more developed and stronger, and their red colours were more pronounced. The males also gave a series of violent shudders and shakes as they released their milt over the eggs in the nest.

One day I ran into one smart trout. Uncle Marc-Aurèle and I had snowshoed in a few miles through the woods from St-Rémi to aptly named Lac de la Truite — Trout Lake. We both chopped holes a few yards from each other and started fishing. I caught a few and missed a few. Then a strange thing happened. Looking down through the hole I saw a trout station itself with its snout about three inches from my hook, stock still except for fins waving gently for stability. I moved the baited hook toward the trout. It backed off, maintaining its three-inch distance. I moved the hook away and the fish moved closer, always keeping the same distance from the hook. Then something happened that really impressed me. Another trout swam in to take the hook, but the sentinel trout wouldn't let it. It chased away the newcomer and again took up its sentinel position. I noticed something different about the sentry. Its mouth was torn and the operculum on one side was protruding at an unnatural angle. The operculum is a hard, cartilage-like lip extending from the tip of the upper jaw along both sides of the mouth. It is somewhat movable and is attached to the mouth by a thin, stretchy membrane. A fish hook through this membrane often tears it, leaving the operculum partly detached from the mouth and sticking out to the side.

The sentinel had obviously been hooked at one time, perhaps by me. It hadn't liked the idea one bit, it seemed, and wouldn't go near the hook again. But more than that, it wouldn't let any other trout near the hook, either. I saw the wounded sentry chase off several fish. There were no more to be caught at this hole, so I went off and chopped another hole a few yards away. Again, I caught some and missed some and then finally that hole dried up, as they all do after a while, so I tramped back to the first hole, flopped down on my belly, and lowered my hook. Immediately, the sentinel was there with its torn operculum, three inches from my hook, chasing away the other fish. I didn't catch another trout in that hole.

Call it what you will — intelligence might be too strong a word for some — but that was one smart trout.

Another trout I hooked one spring day in a brook not far from the village was a different story. It didn't win any prizes for intelligence, in my book. My equipment was simple, as usual — an alder branch with a roll of black line wrapped around the tip. I was using worms for bait. I let my line swirl gradually downstream with the current, then, with an explosive splash, a big fish swallowed the hook, gave a sharp tug, and snapped the damp-rotted line, taking off with my hook, trailing a foot or so of black line from its mouth. Muttering a few choice words, I frantically whipped off some line until I got to a sound section, cut off the rotted part, and tied on a new hook that I baited with a fresh, wiggling worm and again let my line drift downstream with the current. In exactly the same spot as before, another violent tug assaulted my alder branch, only this time the line wasn't rotted and a fine two-and-a-half-pound speckled went flying over my shoulder to do a flopping slide down the steep clay slope behind me. I quickly turned around, crouching like a catcher at home plate, and fielded the squirming fish. I held my prize up to admire it and suddenly did a double take when I saw two lines dangling from the fish's mouth, both mine.

So what do you call that trout, a slow learner?

CHAPTER TEN

THE HUGE TROUT OF TOWER LAKE

ON THE HIGHEST MOUNTAINTOP surrounding St-Rémi there rose — and still rises — a ninety-foot-high fire-lookout tower. It was to this tower that fire marshal René St-Louis hiked every day during periods of high forest-fire risk when the duff underfoot was crunchy and flammable — a six-mile round trip on a very steep trail. It was also to the tower that the young people of the village climbed on sunny days for pleasant summer outings, especially when René St-Louis was not on duty. It was about the only place where boys and girls could be together without the inconvenience of lots of brothers and sisters around, or even worse, parents. Families were big in those days. We boys were very respectful and chivalrous toward the girls, of course, so we let them climb up the tower ladder first as we watched from below. I have to confess that the fact girls wore skirts back then, even on outings to the woods, did not escape the attention of us boys.

Money was scarce in the thirties and early forties, so many mothers made underwear for their children out of the hundred-pound sacks that flour and sugar came in. Bleach faded out the printing on the bags, but there always remained a faint image of lettering on the underwear. When the girls reached a strategic height not very far up the ladder, we boys would crane our necks upward and call out, "Five Roses!" "Robin Hood!" "Redpath!", which naturally elicited shrieks and giggles from the girls as they half-heartedly made pretences of hiding their bare legs — a difficult task since both their hands were occupied with climbing the ladder.

From the top of the tower one could see endless forest and lakes, and if a forest fire started, it was easily detected. Two wires and a telephone connected the tower to the village below to sound the alarm. There was one small lake that could barely be seen from the tower when the leaves were *off* the trees. (It couldn't be seen at all in summer.) The lake nestles fairly close to the base of the mountain on which the tower stands, and so is too close in to get a good clear line of sight to the lake from the tower. Its name is Lac de la Tour — Tower Lake.

It was common knowledge in the village that Tower Lake had no trout swimming in its waters, so no one ever fished it in its off-the-trail location. My uncle, Jean-Marie, and his cousin, Côme, got the idea one day of secretly stocking Tower Lake with speckled trout, keeping quiet about it, and going back in three or four years time to see if the trout had survived, and if so, find out how big they were and catch some. In the spring of the year, my uncle and his cousin set a minnow trap at the outlet of one of the well-known trout lakes about two kilometres from Tower Lake and captured two pails full of fingerling trout. Then the pair quietly bushwhacked through the forest toward Tower Lake, each with a heavy pail in hand, listening intently as they went to make sure no one was in the woods close by. When they reached the shore of Tower Lake, they carefully began releasing the fingerling trout and got the surprise of their lives.

Huge, frenzied trout roiled the water into a froth, gobbling up the fingerlings as soon as they hit the water. It was like the feeding frenzies of trout in the basins of the fish hatchery at St-Faustin. When my uncle and his cousin recovered from their astonishment, they came to the only logical conclusion: the huge trout had been there all the time, but no one had ever fished the lake, because, for some reason or other, common wisdom had always had it that there were no fish in it. The two men didn't have fishing gear with them, so they could not test the waters, so to speak, which sure looked promising. Very carefully, and stopping to listen from time to time, the pair stealthily bushwhacked their way back through the woods to join up with the trail that came down from the fire tower and headed home. More than ever now, they wanted their mission to remain clandestine.

The following day they went back with fishing lines and bait. Alder branches for rods were cut from the brush and they tried their luck, which was not long in coming. They each quickly pulled out five beautiful, splashing, speckled trout, one after the other, and stopped. With the lake being so small, they wanted to limit the number of fish they took out each trip. The fish weighed in at one and a half to two kilos each. Any more would have been wasteful, and besides, they would have been pretty heavy to carry. Discretion became the byword. To be found bushwhacking through the woods with close to ten kilos of fish each would be mighty suspicious.

At nineteen with a mess of speckled trout caught with uncles Jean-Marie on the left and Lucien in the middle, holding Jean-Marie's daughter, Claudette, 1950.

The objective for the return trip was to make it back as secretly as possible through the trackless forest to the trail that came down from the tower. At that point they were safe, because they were then on a trail people also took to reach two other trout lakes higher up, and that joined up with the tower trail. Had they met someone, they would have said that they had had unusually good luck at the higher-up lakes, which everybody knew had trout in them.

Some years later, when I was about nineteen, Uncle Jean-Marie and his brother Lucien, who like others in the immediate family, had been let in on the precious secret, swore me to secrecy and took me up to Tower Lake with the same stealth that they always used to get there. It didn't take long to line up five beauties each on the soft, green moss. My uncle and his cousin usually stuck to their five-fish limit, though sometimes they allowed themselves an extra share as a gift for Curé Allard, the village priest. It couldn't do much harm, and who knew, maybe God would take account of how well they took care of his priest.

Unfortunately, over the years, the secret eventually leaked out and Tower Lake became heavily visited by fishermen from the village. It soon fell to the level of the other trout lakes in the region: fishing was not bad, but nothing magical like it had been. The last time I caught trout there sometime in the late fifties I was with my friend Paul, and we came back with only two fish, one weighing in at one kilo and the other at one and a half kilos, which are quite respectable sizes for speckleds, but never since have I caught another trout in Tower Lake.

CHAPTER ELEVEN
THE PORCUPINE OF LAC CROCHE

THE GREEN MOUNTAIN VALLEYS surrounding St-Rémi cradle many small, crystal-clear lakes whose cold depths are home to speckled trout. Nothing but trout swam in those pure lakes, speckled for the most part, and in the case of a few of the larger lakes there also lived lake trout — the *namaycush* of the First Nations. Three of those lakes were special because they still had old, mossy, woodcutters' log cabins hunkering down on their shores in the thirties and forties. Lac Canon got its name from a deep, perfectly round horizontal hole just about the size of a small cannon-ball mysteriously eroded into the solid-rock face of a cliff overlooking the lake some three or four metres up from the water level; Lac Croche got its name because it is long and "*croche*" — crooked; larger Lac Wagamung, home to both speckled and lake trout, was given its beautiful name long ago by the original inhabitants. The cabins were not big — I had to bend down to go through their doorways. No woodcutters used them anymore, and they had seen better days, but they were still pretty sound. Furniture was Spartan — a wood-burning cookstove, a kitchen table, a couple of chairs, and beds with planks of wood or ancient, bare-metal springs for mattresses. None of the trout lakes around St-Rémi was accessible by car.

Mossy forest trails worn by countless padding feet over the years — four, five, six kilometres long — wound their way through the forest to the shores of these lakes. It was in the cabins of lakes Croche, Canon, and Wagamung that a spark was struck in my soul that was later fanned into flames of passion about wilderness cabins. Some fifty years later, this full-blown passion led me to build my own small log cabin on the shore of Lake of the Old Uncles in the nearby Valley of the Little Nation.

It was to Lac Croche that René St-Louis took me fishing one day. René was the shortest man in St-Rémi — four feet, ten inches. But that didn't mean he wasn't active. He was the fire ranger of the region, and when the risk of fire was high he walked three miles to the fire watchtower, spent the day scanning the woods through his binoculars for smoke, and then walked the three mile trip back. When there was no danger of forest fires, such as after heavy rain storms, René got a respite from his forest-ranger duties and took time off to enjoy himself. He went trout fishing.

A nice thing about village life in those unhurried days was that a boy could often tag along with one of the men when he went fishing. I guess it was because they were both boys at heart when they held a fishing rod.

René was leaving in the early afternoon to spend the night in the old log cabin on the shore of Crooked Lake. I asked if I could go along. "Sure," he said, "Better two men fishing than just one." He knew how to make a boy feel good. I threw together some leftover boiled potatoes to make home fries in a pan, a few tea bags, some bread and butter, a pot of my grandmother's homemade jam, and away we went, bamboo rods over our shoulders. It was a five-kilometre walk from the village to the lake and cabin — one and a half kilometres along the gravel road toward Huberdeau, and three and a half kilometres along a soft, narrow footpath through a mixed hardwood forest to the shores of Crooked Lake.

The fish were hungry and we soon had a good number of beautiful, muscular fish with sparkling, red rubies in cold, steel-blue settings lining their sides — enough for our supper and a few for breakfast. The spring sky was light until nine o'clock on those wonderful, long, spring days. Nightfall in the forest is a magic time. A calm comes over the land, the wind dies away, birdsongs become particularly loud and clear in the evening silence, and as the darkness grows deeper, even the birds settle down and stop singing. Refreshing cool air settles over the forest as night comes on. In the cabin, the yellow light of a candle flickered over us two hungry fishermen as we prepared supper. The main course was cut-up cubes of boiled potatoes fried in butter along with really fresh trout, followed by bread slices toasted on top of the hot cookstove, slathered with butter and jam, all washed down with scalding hot tea. What more could we ask for to appease healthy hungers sharpened by a good hike, fishing, and the cool forest air? No further seasoning was necessary.

After supper, my cabin partner told stories. I never tired of hearing René talk about his life spent rambling the woods. I didn't have to say a word. René had plenty of adventures for both of us. Our natural tiredness helped along by the flickering candlelight and our fully satisfying meal soon put an end to the stories for the night. We pulled on our spare sweaters and crawled onto the bare boards of the wooden bunks, and fell quickly into deep, restful sleep.

A few hours later, I woke up in the darkness of night with a cold foot. Earlier in the day, some water accidentally slopped into one of my boots. With no dry socks to change into, I had gone to bed with one foot wet and the other dry. Well, it gets cool at night on the shores of those trout lakes, even in summer, and my cold, wet foot woke me up. I think having one foot wet and the other dry was worse that having two wet ones.

I suddenly perked up my ears. Something was gnawing. It sounded like an animal in the cabin cutting into some woody morsel with rodent teeth. I knew that porcupines loved to gnaw their way into forest cabins — I had seen some of their work. The last thing I wanted to contend with in the pitch blackness of the cabin was a prickly porcupine. A crawling feeling up the back of my neck made me shiver just thinking there might be one waddling around the cabin floor right then ready to impale me if I stepped on him. Porcupine or not, I had to find out where the gnawing was coming from. Gingerly, I stepped onto the cold floor and slowly, carefully edged my way across it to the table in the centre of the cabin where we had left the candle and some matches, finding them by feel. Fumbling in the dark, I finally got a flame on the candle. Its weak light was less than reassuring. The flickering flame sent dancing shadows everywhere, all of them looking like porcupines.

The gnawing didn't seem to come from the middle of the cabin, where I was. Picking up the candle, I carefully moved straight across over to the other wall opposite the beds. The sound grew fainter. Slowly, inch by inch, I followed the log wall to the corner of the cabin. The sound didn't change much. I turned the corner and followed the wall the stove was on, going around the stove and to the corner of the next wall — the one the bunks were on. The sound seemed to get louder. I carefully followed the edge of the bunks, straining to hear the sound, nerves taut in the wavering candlelight. The gnawing was definitely growing louder. It seemed to be coming from under the bunks, right under where René's inert form lay deep in sleep. Holding the candle, I slowly kneeled down on the floor and examined the space under the bunks by the flickering light, ready to spring back at the sight of a porcupine. Strangely, the sound was not quite as loud down there under the bed. I straightened up my body, but stayed on my knees. The sound grew louder. I pushed the candle closer to René's sleeping body. The sound seemed to be coming from René's bed. In fact it *was* coming from René's bed. As I held the candle close to René's face, I could see his jaw muscles tightening, moving, relaxing, tightening. There was my porcupine, grinding his teeth in his sleep. Some porcupine!

CHAPTER TWELVE

THE GREEN BOTTLE

THERE WAS ONE LAKE IN particular my uncles would retreat to when the fall fishing fit was upon them. Uncle Jean-Marie confessed to me one day while we were fishing that he could never resist the siren call of catching trout when the forest started to turn red in the fall. The temple of fall fishing for Jean-Marie was near a neighboring village at Lac Rognon — Kidney Lake (so named because it was in the shape of two side-by-side kidneys connected at their middles by a narrow passage of open water.)

When I saw Uncle Jean-Marie get out the bottle of John de Kuyper's Genever gin in late summer or early fall, I knew he was going fishing with one or two of the other village men. He never drank alcohol on any other occasion. I also knew, though, that I wasn't going with them. It wasn't that my uncle didn't take me fishing. He did — often. We caught an awful lot of speckled trout together. But when he got out the bottle of gin — *gros gin*, we called it in French — I knew he was getting ready to go to Lac Rognon with his cousin Côme, or some friends, and that I would be staying home.

Lac Rognon was kind of special. It was one of the few lakes in the hills near St-Rémi D'Amherst that were home to both lake trout and speckled trout. I had never been there, though. When my uncle and his fellow fishermen went there, it was always overnight, staying in an old woodcutters' log cabin on the shore of the lake. They always brought back fish, too: big lake trout — ten-, twelve-pound fish — much bigger than the speckled trout I caught.

How I envied them. Lac Rognon seemed a magical place, with huge trout swimming in its mysterious depths. To spend a night in the solitary old log cabin on its shores after drinking *gros gin* and catching fish all day became an almost unattainable boyhood dream for me. Oh, how I wished I could have gone with them, but for a reason that I didn't fathom at the time, I couldn't. A fourteen-year-old just didn't seem welcome. I was sure it had something to do with the gin. I vowed to find out.

Many times when I had been down in the dank, dirt-floor cellar under my uncle's inn (he had bought it from his father), I had examined the dusty racks draped in cobwebs holding his store of liquor bottles. I knew exactly where to look. There were brown bottles of scotch and rye, clear bottles of dry gin and rum, and assorted bottles of various other lesser liquors. But those bottles held no fascination for me. It was the dark, transparent green of the Genever gin bottles that flashed with special magic in the flickering light of my candle.

On an August afternoon, I sneaked into the cellar and picked out a small, ten-ounce, green flask, blew off the dust and spider webs, and examined it closely in the weak light of the candle to make sure it was *gros gin*. I carefully hid it in my shoulder pack next to some worms and a ham sandwich, and slipped out the exterior door of the dingy cellar into the blinding sunlight. Shouldering my bamboo fishing pole, which was in the back shed, I headed for the hilly woods half a mile behind the inn. I, too, would know the magic of drinking gin and catching trout on the shore of a wilderness lake, even if I had to do it alone.

I entered the woods and, after three kilometres padding along a soft forest trail past First and Second lakes, reached the shores of big Lac Wagamung. There, I set my pack with its precious contents carefully down on the ground, got out my fishing gear, and tied a hook and a lead sinker to the black line at the end of my bamboo rod. I whipped my rod back over my head and then sharply forward, casting the wriggling worm on a hook into the dark, green water. I put a cork bobber on the line to let me know when a fish gobbled up the worm, and jammed the big end of the rod into a crevice in the rock.

Carefully, I took the green bottle from the pack and held it up to the light, the better to appreciate the cold, emerald sparkle of the glass. Such a moment was to be savoured and not rushed. The magic started to take hold. A fleeting moment of panic seized me when the black composition cover wouldn't come off, but then it suddenly released with a sharp crack. I twisted it off and held the bottle to my nose. The strong vapours invaded my nostrils. The smell was not quite what I had expected. It was a strong smell, like old wooden barrels that had been around for a while. I guessed the smell came from the old oaken casks that the gin was aged in.

Suddenly, the float bobbed crazily up and down and then headed for the depths. Quickly but carefully, I screwed the cover back onto the bottle and laid it aside on the moss. I grabbed the bamboo pole and gave it a strong pull. A fat speckled trout flew over my head and lay flopping on the smooth rock behind me. I mercifully dispatched the struggling fish with a sharp blow on the head from a stick, and laid the trout in the shade, covering it over with wet moss. The magic was increasing.

I cast the line back into the water with a new, vigorously protesting worm on the hook. Back to the gin. I screwed off the black cap once more and again inhaled the volatile vapours. They hadn't changed. I pressed my lips to the mouth of the flask and tilted it back, taking a gulp. The burning liquid fairly burst from my lips in an explosion of alcoholic spray. My God, but it was awful! When my coughing calmed down, I lifted the bottle and examined it to see if I had not picked up a bottle of turpentine by mistake. It was gin all right. As the burning feeling subsided, it was replaced by a sort of warm feeling and the aftertaste did have a certain quality to it that had been masked by the initial searing shock.

"Maybe it takes some getting used to," I thought. "I'll take smaller sips."

Again, I lifted the bottle to my lips and let a bit of gin trickle into my mouth, screwed up my eyes, and swallowed hard. It really didn't taste any better, but at least I was able to swallow it and hold it down. I shuddered as it burned its way down my throat. A few seconds later that warm feeling came over me again. I took another sip, and then another. As sip succeeded sip, the warm feeling grew stronger. I looked sideways at the bottle. It was almost half gone. And then, gradually, I felt a change coming over me. That warm feeling was turning into something different, something ugly. It was turning into a sickening merry-go-round whirl. Round and round went the world. I lay down on the rock, but the merry-go-round only turned faster. I got up again. The feeling wasn't quite as bad when I stood, but, oh God! how I wished to be close to my bed at home.

I didn't even bother to roll up the line. It just stayed there — and the trout, too. God knows why, but I stuffed the half-empty bottle back into my pack before staggering down the trail to the village. Walking was rough, but stopping was even rougher. Once I made the mistake of lying down to rest, and that sickening merry-go-round started spinning again. I struggled to my feet and wavered down the path. Lord, if I could only reach my bed. I was terrified of meeting someone in the village, but luck was with me. It was suppertime and everyone was at the table. That's the way it was in those days. The church bell tolled the *angélus*, six o'clock sharp, and everyone in the village sat down to supper. I made it back to the inn without seeing a soul.

I was anxious to sneak up the back way to my room unseen. But first, there was one task left to do. The terrible evidence had to be got rid of. I cursed myself for bringing back that half-full bottle. But I had. And now, how to get rid of it. In the semi-darkness of the back shed was a round-nosed shovel with a long, straight handle. I took it along the fence that ran down the side of the shed to the fourth post from the corner — it was hidden from the view of anyone in the inn. Fourth post from the corner. For some unfathomable reason I still don't understand, it seemed important to remember where the bottle was going to be buried. Lord knows I had no intention of using it again. When the job was done I felt relief at being free of the cursed thing. I staggered to my room on the third floor of the inn and collapsed on the bed. The terrible merry-go-round started up again. Round and round spun the room. Round and round spun my stomach. The result was inevitable: I stumbled to the washroom and heaved up what was left of the gin and staggered back to my bed. The world slowed down and stopped whirling after a time and I fell into a deep sleep.

Waking up the next morning was rough. My head was throbbing. I really worried why no one seemed to have wondered where I was at suppertime last night. And if they were wondering, what could I tell them?

When I felt I could stand up without my head splitting open, I gingerly stepped my way downstairs to the kitchen. Aunt Pauline spotted me.

"Gerard! You look terrible. Where were you? We were worried about you last night. We didn't see you come home. Uncle Jean-Marie checked your room after supper and saw that you were asleep. My, but you don't look well."

I didn't doubt that I looked unwell. Suddenly, I saw my way out.

"Oh! I don't feel too well, all right. But I feel better now than I felt last night." I wasn't lying. "I had indigestion last night, so I didn't come to supper. But I'm feeling better this morning." My story may have lacked a few details, but basically, it was the truth, and it was believed, for no one could have possibly imagined what I had really been up to. Erroneously, as it turned out, they had the utmost confidence in me.

Although my urge to fish was still intact, never again did I feel the desire to drink Genever gin, or any other liquor for that matter, while fishing.

Some forty odd years later, the sun was low in the sky on a clear evening in late August. It was also in August that I had buried the bottle at the base of the fourth fencepost from the corner to hide the evidence. It intrigued me to know if the bottle was still there. If I didn't look now, I would never find it because the fence was going to be torn down the following week and the benchmark fourth post, along with all the other posts, would be gone. In the back shed was the same shovel I had used to bury it — the shovel that was almost as long as I was tall when I last used it on that long-ago day. Now it only came up to the grey whiskers on my chin.

I carried the shovel to the base of the fourth post. Gently, I leaned the nose of the shovel on the ground and gingerly pushed it in with my foot. Memory can play tricks with the passage of time. I knew pretty well where the spot was, but this was no time to be careless. The bottle wasn't deep, and after only the second gentle prod with the shovel, I nudged it. Down on my knees, I brushed away the clinging earth, gently lifted the flask out of the ground, and held it up to the rays of the dying sun. The black composition cover was intact and it was still half full of liquid, just as I had left it forty years before.

It was that magic time in the evening when sounds fall away to a hush, just before darkness ushers in the close of day. I remembered that other magic — imagined magic many years ago that turned out to be bad magic. The emerald colour of the glass was still there, but it seemed dull and the sparkle was gone. I screwed off the cap. One last time, I lifted the flask to my lips and drank a toast to my youth of those bygone days. The liquid still burned. I shuddered as it seared its way down my throat. Then the warm feeling came on. Not much change there. But what a world of other changes had occurred in me, and in the world around me, between this sip and the last one I had taken from the flask on the shores of Lac Wagamung forty years before. I screwed the top back on and gently laid the half-empty bottle back on its side in the earth. Carefully, I shovelled dirt into the hole and softly tamped it down with my boot.

The mountains surrounding the village were all dark now. I turned to go. A short, quick tremor shivered my shoulders. "The evening chill," I thought, as I glanced up at the crisp, clear sky. Fall is in the air already."

A week later the fence was taken down and the location of the bottle was lost forever. It's probably still there, where the fourth post from the corner used to be, but I couldn't ever find it now.

CHAPTER THIRTEEN

UNCLE LUCIEN'S LESSON

UNCLE LUCIEN'S LESSON had nothing to do with fishing. Lucien knew that teaching me about fishing was very important for my enjoyment of life as a young man, but he also knew there were other lessons about nature that were important for a young man to learn.

Every year at the beginning of September I went back to Brooklyn to start the school year, and every year in the first days of July I came back to St-Rémi for the summer. The year I turned fifteen, I was more eager than usual to get back to St-Rémi at the end of the school year. It had something to do with Ghislaine, a girl my age. I had met Ghislaine the previous summer and, for reasons I didn't fully appreciate yet, I had found her particularly interesting and was looking forward to seeing her again. We got together soon after I arrived from the city and found that we really liked being together. I didn't neglect my fishing, but being with Ghislaine became very important, too, and we spent the summer developing our friendship.

By the time we both turned fifteen that summer, we found that the bonds of friendship had grown stronger over the months of absence. As I said before, there was one factor that stood in the way of young love in those days in St-Rémi, and that was how awfully hard it was for young people to be alone together, what with crowds of siblings, parents, and relatives always in evidence at home. One way to achieve a bit of intimate aloneness in a rural village was to go for long walks in the evening along the dark streets, arms around each other's waists and holding hands. There was no electricity in the village yet and the streets were very, very dark, especially when there was no moon. One moonless evening, as Ghislaine and I happened to stroll past Uncle Lucien's house on one of our walks, it started to rain. Although Lucien could not see us as he sat rocking in the dark on his porch, he heard us talking and correctly guessed who we were.

"Come up on the porch and get out of the rain," he called out through the darkness. We gratefully accepted his hospitality. After a few moments he suggested, "Come inside. It will be a little cool outside with this rain." So we moved into his living room, where he sat us down on a sofa, lit one kerosene lamp with the flame set low, and promptly went upstairs to join his wife Yvette, already in bed for the night.

That evening, on the sofa in Lucien's living room, unfettered nature took its course. Ghislaine and I both discovered for the first time in our lives the delectable pleasure of kissing. It was extremely difficult to take leave of each other that evening after Uncle Lucien's lesson. We learned the true meaning of "parting is such sweet sorrow."

Although Lucien knew well what he was doing, I was certain that Aunt Yvette would not have approved back then in the forties.

Six years ago, old Uncle Lucien left this world after a long and happy life. At his funeral, I spoke with his wife, Aunt Yvette, who was then in her 80s, and I told her about Lucien's lesson back then in the forties, and what had happened one summer evening in her living room as she slept, blissfully unaware, upstairs on the floor above us. I waited a bit anxiously for her reaction. She thought about it for a long moment, then looked up at me with a smile. "He did well," she said.

CHAPTER FOURTEEN

FINDING MY FIRST LAKE

HAVING BEEN BORN IN the Laurentian Hills, I am really at home in the mountains. There is great pleasure of anticipation when bushwhacking over a forest hill or mountain for the first time, a feeling that drives one to reach the summit, even if it is only to discover that there is just another mountain on the other side. But if a lake, never seen before, comes into view, a thrill of discovery shivers through my body when I see the sparkling blue surface far below through the branches. Very often a map has already told me of the lake, but when I have never been there before, the thrill is not less for having known of its existence beforehand from the map. Seeing, and even drinking from it, or swimming in it, is far more than merely knowing that it is there. In Walden, Thoreau writes,

> A lake is the landscape's most beautiful and expressive feature. It is earth's eye, looking into which the beholder measures the depth of his own nature.

More than once, finding such a new lake has resulted in the further pleasure of making a fine catch of speckled trout.

The thrill of finding my first lake by map and compass is unforgettable. It may not have been a great feat of exploration; I had been within a few hundred yards of this pond many times when in the forest, never suspecting its existence. When my uncles took me fishing, it was always to lakes that the villagers had known for many years and there were well-worn footpaths leading to them. They never used a compass, even when hunting through the trackless forest, because they were familiar with every square metre of the woods around St-Rémi. Not needing a compass, they never learned how to use one. I was not as familiar with the forest as they were, so as I grew older, I bought a compass to find my way around and taught myself how to use it, together with a topographic map, when navigating the unknown forest.

Montreal was my home at the time my fascination led me to try map and compass orienteering. On the slope of Mount Royal sits the University of Montreal, with a tall, concrete tower reaching for the sky. It is visible for quite a distance, but I decided to "find" it by map and compass. It didn't matter much that I could see the tower. I pretended I couldn't, and visually ignored it. Starting from my home, I would "find" the tower. After buying my compass, I had learned about declination, which has to do with the fact that a compass does not point exactly to true north, but rather to magnetic north. I also learned about latitudes and longitudes and what they meant on a map. I was ready to "explore."

On the city map I was using, I spotted where I was starting out from: my home address. The university tower also appeared on the map. I drew a straight line between the two points and, with a protractor, measured the angle that I would have to set on my compass to "find" the tower, correcting for declination. The situation had a certain realism in that I could not follow a straight line to the tower because "valleys," called "streets," got in my way and I had to follow them. I did some dead reckoning to account for the fact that I was jogging around corners, and after walking a few kilometres, lo and behold! there was the tower looming over me. I felt a great sense of new-found power. The wilderness beckoned!

The next time I went to Lac Croche fishing with Uncle Jean-Marie, I took a topographical map and my compass with me. On the map, I had noticed a small pond a few hundred yards off to the side of Lac Croche. Its existence was unknown to me until I saw it on the map, even though I had been to the area many times. After arriving at Lac Croche, I parted with my uncle, telling him that I was going to use my compass to find the pond

... which he knew full well was there, and had dismissed as insignificant since there were no fish in it. To me, it was full of significance, because it represented a challenge, which, if responded to correctly, would mean I'd find my first wilderness pond with my own resources — a powerful result indeed at that stage of my wilderness capabilities. I had drawn a line from Lac Croche to the pond on the map, measured the degrees of heading, and, correcting it for declination, set it on my compass.

In a few hundred yards, a blue, sparkling reflection danced before my eyes through the branches. It was just a shallow, weedy pond, and quite obviously did not harbour any trout, but no matter — I had found it myself! Once again, I felt the rush of my new-found power — in the wilderness this time. And so began a lifetime of map-and-compass bushwhacking through trackless forest in search of unknown lakes and, hopefully, the ultimate trout. I did find some big ones.

Part Three

WILD CABINS
I HAVE KNOWN

IN MY YEARS OF WILDERNESS rambling, I have run into quite a number of wild cabins. A wild cabin to me is one that is surrounded by forest and can't be reached by car — only by canoe or on foot. The three cabins near St-Rémi on lakes Cannon, Croche, and Wagamung fit into that category. Days and nights spent in those cabins on the shores of pristine mountain lakes in my impressionable youth gave a bent to my spirit that has lasted until my elder years and without a doubt will be with me as long as I live. Through the years I have discovered other wild cabins, most of which have given me great pleasure; a few, great sorrow in the case of those that were destroyed or damaged by the irrational hand of man. The following stories are about some of these cabins.

CHAPTER ONE

PHILOSOPHY CABIN

IT WASN'T A PRETTY CABIN that Doug and I had found. Not at all. It was really a makeshift affair, not made to last many years — probably only as long as it took to log the surrounding forest in some distant past. Its simple plank construction lacked the nobility of a log cabin. But somehow it still clung to life despite its obvious age and a flat roof that was never made to support the snows of many winters. One of the roof beams had cracked badly and a couple of more recent posts had been added on the inside, from floor to ceiling, to support it.

The door of the cabin faced the wrong direction, so all the winter snows piled their highest drifts right in front of it. On top of that, the door opened outwards, so to get in we had to use a snowshoe to shovel out a pit around the door. At one end of the cabin there had been a one-horse stall years ago with a low wall of planks separating it from the rest of the structure. The heat generated by the horse would have been appreciated by the woodcutters on bitter-cold nights. Most of the separating planks had long since been removed, probably by later users of the cabin to fuel the rusty forty-five-gallon oil drum that served as a stove. Throughout the years, this old stove had probably revived many sets of numb fingers and

Courtesy of Elaine Kenney.

"Philosophy Cabin"

Elaine's sketch of Philosophy Cabin.

toes, but in recent times my friend Doug and I were the only ones who shared its warmth.

We had stumbled upon the abandoned cabin by accident one cold December morning while on a snowshoe ramble. It was pretty obvious that it had lost its usefulness to its former owners as it gathered moss and slowly aged in the thick evergreens. But the loneliness of the cabin and its surroundings only increased its value to us as a haven of quietude in this otherwise unquiet world. We started using it as a kind of retreat.

In winter — a fine time for using wild cabins — when the snow lay four feet deep, we had to snowshoe up a kilometre-and-a-half hill to reach a level path that, after a couple of kilometres more, dropped into a fir and spruce valley that secretly cradled the cabin in the shadows of its tall spires. A crystalline brook trickled into the valley even on the coldest, most bitter day in January. To reach the pure, icy liquid, it was best to be two — one stretching out on his belly down the four-foot crevice in the snow, the other hanging on to his boots to prevent him from falling in.

Many Saturday mornings, Doug and I tramped up on snowshoes through the beech-and-maple forest that led to the valley. The first task when we arrived at the cabin was scooping away the snow from its misplaced door. Then came the sawing and splitting of dead trees to feed the rusty, ravenous, forty-five-gallon drum.

We drew water from the icy brook to brew up steaming cups of coffee. Lunch, which was most likely a stew or sometimes chilli, soon simmered and bubbled on the radiating metal top of the barrel, while a few swigs of French-Canadian *caribou* — a mix of pure-grain whiskey and red wine — combined with the winter cold and exercise to produce monstrous appetites. Then, round-bellied and suffused with warmth, *caribou*, and satisfaction, we leaned back on the old, rickety chairs, and let the unique power of the cabin gradually overtake us. We named it Philosophy Cabin because, in its conducive atmosphere, we discussed and explored endless important philosophical issues and solved many of the world's problems. Words and thoughts emerged in that hallowed hall that we were sure would have remained unborn in the very serious, civilized world not so far away.

Doug and I were, and still are, good friends, the kind you only have a very few of in a lifetime. In Philosophy Cabin we became better friends. In the warmth of the crackling fire deep in the evergreen valley, the bonds of friendship grew stronger. Thoughts flowed with ease and freedom and we learned more about each other's inner beings than it seemed the city below would have permitted. We were reminded of an old Indian who once said, "I don't believe I could think straight in a city." We understood what he meant.

"Whose cabin is it?" someone once asked.

"It's ours," we replied.

Perhaps according to the books of the county clerk we had lied, but in our own books, it was ours. After all, we were the only ones using it. Never did we see another track leading to it. We also "owned" Philosophy Lake nearby — though it was really a shallow and rather weedy pond. We "owned" Philosophy River, our trickling brook. We needed no deed. It was enough to know that all these things belonged to us — the cabin, the brook, the pond, the forest, the swamp — in a way that had nothing to do with ownership, and that no deed could ever enhance.

CHAPTER TWO
THE CABIN ON THE JESUIT PASSAGE

ONE HUNDRED AND TWENTY miles north of Quebec City lies a large lake called Lac St-Jean (Lake Saint John). Many centuries ago, Lac St-Jean must have been connected to the sea, because a beautiful and combative landlocked salmon, Ouananiche, swims in its frigid depths. Today, the town of Metabetchouan lies at the south end of the lake. It started out in the late 1600s as a fur-trading post and Jesuit mission hacked out of the northern forest. The fur traders brought in useful goods that the Montagnais Indians of the region needed, in return for furs, and the Jesuit missionaries brought the native inhabitants the Catholic religion.

There were two routes to reach Metabetchouan from Quebec City in those days: a winter one, called the Jesuit Trail, which took advantage of frozen lakes and swamps for snowshoeing, and a summer one, the Jesuit Passage, which was somewhat longer, but took advantage of many miles of canoeable lakes, rivers, and streams.

Two main rivers were used by those who followed the Jesuit Passage. First, the Jacques Cartier, which the Jesuits and traders ascended from the Quebec City end to the long and sinuous Lac Henri Mercier. From there, they crossed over to the watershed of the Metabetchouan River,

Doug Dacres on the porch of Jesuit Passage cabin, 1969.

whose north-flowing waters led the missionaries to the trading post of the same name on Lac St-Jean.

On a weekend in the late sixties, Doug and I canoed some forty-two kilometres of the Jesuit Passage in its northern reaches. We were intrigued by the fascinating history of the Passage and decided to investigate the possibility of being able to canoe and portage its full length of some two hundred kilometres. Since the Jesuit Passage wound its way through Parc des Laurentides for part of its length, our first point of contact was the Parks Service of Quebec. There, we met a most obliging Mr. Benjamin Balatti, who became very interested in our project. He suggested that if the way through was still practical, the historical Passage could perhaps be declared an official canoe route of the Province of Quebec. One consideration, he cautioned, was that the part of the park we wanted to traverse was not open to the public at the time, but he said that would not be a problem. He assured us that, since we would be doing this work in collaboration with the Parks Service, he would provide us with a special permit to be in that part of the park.

Mr. Balatti gave us a copy of a primitive map of the area dating back to the seventeenth century that singled out stands of larch, or "tamarac" as it is also called, with several notations of "good tamarac" marked on it. The early surveyors were interested in tamarac because of its hardness and good rot-resisting qualities. Preliminary plans for developing a woodcutting operation had been laid, and tamarac was to be used to build a wooden railway to take out the logs, probably by horse power. These plans were never implemented, but the map served us well.

We decided to attack our project in stages since our jobs at the time did not permit us to be absent for the entire period required to explore the whole Passage in one shot. Our homes were in Quebec City in 1969, so it was decided to start with the southern part of the route, which was close by.

We launched our canoe in the Jacques Cartier River some forty kilometres north of Quebec City on a cloudy July 5th in 1969. The surface of the river fizzed gently as grey skies drizzled their wetness down on us. It seemed like the whole world was shrouded in a dripping mantle of low-lying clouds. Huddling under the semi-protection of our ponchos, we were not immune from the searching drops, which eventually found and invaded every centimetre of our skin. By moving as little as possible, we kept the cold morning air from slipping in between skin and wet clothing. We paddled all day in silence with short, clipped strokes, pulled by muscles tight with cold. By late afternoon, the Jacques Cartier River was still quite wide, but the shores were drawing closer together as we pushed upstream. The quickening flow was beginning to require more effort from our cold, cramped muscles to drive the canoe against the current, which helped to warm us up some. A few hundred yards ahead through the misty air, we saw a white spot in the river that signalled a rapid where the nervous river tumbled out of the hills. Pulling strongly on our paddles, we approached the boiling water, turned toward shore, and beached our canoe on the pebbly beach. Doug slowly turned and sat there for a moment, hunched over, peering misery at me through the curtain of drops dripping off the peak of his soggy cap. Our stiff bodies slowly uncoiled with shudders and tremors as the parting of skin and drenched cloth sucked the cold air in to wash over our clammy goose bumps.

We hoped the dancing rapid would provide supper — our light pack contained little food, just a few potatoes, and some year-old beef jerky in case the trout we were counting on refused to rise. Doug, carefully picking his way along the slippery rocks lining the throat of splashing foam, looked for a portage trail while I teased the swirling eddies at the foot of the rapids with rod and fly. It was a relief to see the fish co-operating. Six speckled trout soon lay glistening on the rocks. There were not too many things going for us, and munching on year-old jerky for supper would not have helped our spirits.

Doug found the portage. It was not a long one — about fifteen hundred feet, starting on the right shore, some one hundred feet below the foot of the rapid. With a quick jerk, he hoisted the canoe onto his shoulders and shuffled up the muddy trail. I trudged behind him with the trout and our single pack. My thoughts wandered back to the days when the Jesuits and their Montagnais guides struggled over this very same trail to get from Quebec City to Lac St-Jean on their mission to bring religion to the Montagnais. I pictured the priests in their floor-length black cassocks and round hats with wide rims picking their way carefully over the slippery rocks with hoisted skirts, but quickly abandoned my own imagery as being impractical. They must have worn more appropriate clothes to travel. I was sharply awakened from my reverie by a slippery patch of mud, which threw me down on all fours. The heavy pack slid to one side and dragged me down into the muck with it. Before, I was only wet. Now I was wet and muddy.

Doug had set the canoe down a few minutes before I arrived at the head of the rapid. We broke off some alder branches to keep the pack out of the bilge water in the bottom of the canoe. Over the pack, we draped and tucked a tarpaulin, which would soon also serve as our shelter for the night when we made camp.

The chill of approaching evening started making its presence felt on our wet backs as we stiffly paddled away from the portage. We knew we would have to stop soon and set up a camp site. I didn't look forward to that. The forest floor was soaked. Our clothes were sopping. Firewood would be drenched. And on top of it all, an evening wind started blowing as the rain still fell. I looked at Doug and asked, "Why do we do this to ourselves? We could be drinking beer, watching TV in your warm living room." Doug smiled under the dripping visor of his poncho and I smiled back at him. It is our standing joke under such conditions, much like Sigurd Olson and his canoeing partners would say to each other in similar situations, "I've been happier, but I can't remember where."

Through the gathering dusk ahead, the white froth of a riffle betrayed another narrowing of the Jacques Cartier. A wide, stony shore bordered the flow on the right as the river curved to that side and disappeared from view around a bend. We tracked the canoe around the inner curve with some fifteen centimetres of water lapping up the sides of our boots. Soaking as we were from head to toe, for some reason it still seemed important to try to keep the water from spilling in over the tops of our boots.

Before tracking up the riffle, we agreed to set up camp at the first suitable spot we found past the bend. Hunched over, we trudged, pushing and pulling the canoe around the rocky bend, crooking our necks at a sharp up-angle to peer ahead through the rain. A certain unnaturalness seemed to dimly come into and out of focus through the grey mist ahead of us as we squinted and blinked to clear our eyes of rainwater. An undefined form was slowly taking shape as we plodded closer. We stared stupidly at first, not believing what our eyes were trying to tell us, but then suddenly, with a rush, it hit us that the dim shape in the mist was a small log cabin! But wait, we thought. Maybe there are only four walls left. Maybe the roof has long ago disintegrated. We ran and slithered and fell in our urgency to see. Bursting in through the door, we were met with blessed dryness. The roof was sound. In one corner was an old wood-burning cookstove, and beside it, a supply of firewood, kindling, and birch bark that only needed the touch of a match to bring it crackling to life in the firebox. Bedding was hung on a rope strung from front to back of the cabin to keep it out of the reach of mice — not quite successfully, as we found out later. We loaded the stove with bark and wood, struck a match, and soon had a roaring fire.

Our extraordinary luck in finding this tight, dry cabin worked a tremendous change in our outlook. Although still sopping wet, we knew that in a very short time our clothes would be steaming and drying around the stove, our skin tingling from a vigorous towel rub, and our bellies full.

The cabin was soon filled with the delicious smells of supper cooking — boiling potatoes, six speckled trout slowly frying to a crisp turn, bannock baking in a frying pan, and a steaming pot of coffee. Our bellies were soon round with satisfaction. A king in his palace could not have been happier.

After supper, in a dry change of clothes, warm, and full of food, we took the time to examine more closely our shelter for the night. It wasn't big — about three and a half metres by four — but was solidly made of round logs, probably spruce or fir, carefully notched in the corners and topped with a sound roof covered with tin. The cabin was not that old and had been built, we found out later, for the park rangers. There were two windows, one in the front wall that the table was pushed up against overlooking the river, the other in a side wall. The door to the outside opened onto a small, covered porch with an old ice box on it to keep food in. There was no other place in the world we wanted to be that night. We soon succumbed to a powerful drowsiness. A family of deer mice urgently abandoned their sanctuary in the mattresses when we pulled them from the overhead rope, laid our sleeping bags on them, and collapsed heavily into bed.

Few pleasures can equal the feelings of satisfaction and security we felt that night, rain drumming gently on the roof, crackling fire casting dancing shadows on the walls and ceiling as we faded into unconsciousness and blissful oblivion in the warmth and dryness of our humble refuge on the Jesuit Passage. It is a marvel what a small weather-tight log cabin in the wilderness can do for one's well-being and security compared to what our alternative would have been: a sopping-wet campsite with just a tarpaulin crackling in the breeze for shelter.

The following morning dawned sunny and dry. We continued our exploration, portaging into long and narrow Lac Henri Mercier, paddling to its end four miles away where we ran out of water to paddle in. The next stage would have been a long portage over the height of land to Lac aux Rognons (Kidney Lake), but we left that for another time and turned for home. Unfortunately, my work required me to leave Quebec City soon after, and Doug and I never did get to finish our exploration of the Jesuit Passage, but we still fondly remember being rescued from a wet, cold night under a tarpaulin by a log cabin on the shore of the Jacques Cartier River.

CHAPTER THREE

THE HOLMES LAKE CABIN

PORTNEUF RESERVE, SOME one hundred kilometres northwest of Quebec City, is an extensive area of forest containing many lakes and several rivers that are ideal for three- and four-day canoe-camping trips. There are a number of old log cabins of varying sizes that can be rented from the Quebec government on several lakes in the reserve for quiet weekends and holidays in wilderness settings. Although the reserve is relatively close to a major city, I have run into very few people when paddling there. Two of the old cabins in the reserve were particularly interesting to Doug and me because they met our definition of wild cabins: there was no automobile access to them and no electricity. These cabins were not part of the government renting scheme, because they were not reachable by car and did not have any of the amenities of civilization, which was just what we were looking for. When enjoying these two cabins, we have always had them to ourselves.

One of the cabins was on a small pond called Holmes Lake. It is on a canoe route that goes by the intriguing name of La Rivière au Lard — the Lard River. We never ran into other campers there — probably due to the twelve portages in the circuit, some of which are a kilometre or two in length. Longish portages eliminate many potential users and make for peaceful and quiet paddling on the connecting lakes and rivers.

The first day of this circuit, which requires hours of paddling and portaging, takes us to Holmes Lake for our first layover. Tucked away into a corner of the pond, where it flows into a stream leading to long and narrow Lard Lake, is the smallest cabin I have ever slept in. It is made of planks, not logs, and is plain and utilitarian as a shelter. We have no quarrels with that. Whenever we do the Lard River circuit, we look forward to its silent welcome at the

Doug relaxing at tiny Holmes Lake cabin after a hard day's canoeing and portaging, 1996.

end of our first day of paddling with as much enthusiasm as if it were a palace — probably more.

A defining feature of the Holmes Lake cabin is that it has only one single-bed-sized bunk with a good, thick mattress to sleep on, and not even enough floor space left over for building a second bunk if one wanted to. This causes a problem, which is really only minor in nature, that one of us has to sleep on the few remaining square centimetres of floor.

Several years ago, on the very first trip we ever made on the Lard River circuit, Doug and I flipped a coin to see who would sleep on the bunk and who on the floor. I don't remember who won, but ever since we have scrupulously remembered who the previous trip's occupant of the bunk was and we have swapped our sleeping arrangements accordingly each time, with one exception. That one exception came about when Doug strained his back lifting his backpack on the very first day of one of our Lard River trips. I ceded my rightful claim to the bed and mattress that night to my suffering partner. I didn't miss my chance to rib Doug though, especially when he seemed to bounce back quite rapidly from his infirmity in about a day and a half. I still rib him about it each time we sleep in the Holmes Lake cabin, and probably always will. It has become a feature of our Lard River trips. But Doug has never strained his back since. It is his turn to sleep on the floor next time.

CHAPTER FOUR

ONE CABIN TOO MANY

THE SECOND PORTNEUF RESERVE cabin we have enjoyed was on Lac Lapeyrère, the largest lake in the reserve and the departure point for a number of canoe circuits, including the Lard River circuit. There is also a relatively easy circuit that starts off in Lac Lapeyrère called the Lac Fou or Crazy Lake circuit, which can be done in one day, but which we usually do in two days, or three if we are really lazy and the weather is good. The circuit consists of a paddle down to the south end of long Lac Lapeyrère, a portage to a stream that takes us to the Crazy Lake portage, another portage to the lake, a paddle through Crazy Lake to a portage trail back down to Lac Lapeyrère, and finally a paddle back to where we parked our car at the start of the circuit. That's if we were to do it in one day, which we have never done, preferring to take our time and camp one or more additional nights on Lac Lapeyrère.

The very first time I did this circuit with Doug about twenty years ago, we discovered a feature of the trip, of which we had not been aware when we left, that immediately made us lazy. Halfway down the first leg of the circuit — the paddle to the end of Lac Lapeyrère — we rounded a point and quite suddenly discovered a wild log cabin on shore that turned out to

be inaccessible except by canoe, or on skis in wintertime. Right then and there we decided to set up camp in the cabin for the night, even though it was still early afternoon. We could not pass it up.

The cabin was set back from the lake about thirty feet on a slope so that the front porch was supported by posts about four or five feet off the ground. There was a window in the front wall and a door that opened out onto a beautiful view of the lake. The logs fit perfectly with each other and the notches were tight. The builder of the cabin had ob-

Doug enjoying One-Too-Many-Cabin for the last time before it was burnt to the ground, 1992.

viously known what he was doing. It was sound and squarely built. During the night it rained and we found out that the roof was tight as well. Of furniture there was none except a wood-burning stove, but that was all right with us. The floor served us well to lay out our air mattresses and sleeping bags and a log bench on the porch was our sofa. We were extremely pleased to discover yet a second wild cabin in Portneuf Reserve.

The second day, we continued paddling on down Lac Lapeyrère to the stream that leads to the Crazy Lake portage trail. We reached the lake and paddled down its length to the portage trail back to Lac Lapeyrère. At this point, we had two choices: we could paddle north to our original point of departure and head on home, or we could paddle south a short distance to the cabin and spend the night there, going north to our departure the following day. I said that the sight of the cabin had made us lazy, so we stayed another night, just for the pleasure of it, and went home the following day.

We had so enjoyed our stay in the cabin that, the subsequent year, Doug and I decided to take a few days in the fall to once again enjoy its comforts. When we paddled around the point behind which lay the cabin, we felt at first that we must be in the wrong place — we could not see the cabin. But as we got closer, we realized that we were indeed at the right place. What we discovered, to our dismay, was that the cabin had burned to the ground. We were tremendously disappointed and sad to find that the cabin no longer existed. We camped at the spot anyway and completed the Crazy Lake circuit the following day, but our hearts were not as joyful as they usually are when we are on a canoe trip.

Several years later, when canoeing in the same area, we met a reserve worker and asked him if he knew what had happened to the cabin and if anybody had been hurt or killed in the fire. We could hardly believe his response.

"No. No one was hurt or killed. It was a well-controlled fire," he said.

"What do you mean by a 'controlled' fire?" I asked

"Well, I mean that when the men set the fire, they were ready to make sure it didn't spread."

"The men? What men?" I prodded.

His next words shocked us.

"The men from the Parks Service."

"The men from the Parks Service?" I asked incredulously. "They set the cabin on fire? On purpose? But why? Why?"

"Well, it was too much trouble to maintain the cabin because there was no way to get to it except by boat."

"But you have a boat," I pressed on.

"I didn't make the decision. It came from headquarters. They decided to burn it down so they wouldn't have to maintain it."

We were completely shocked. I could see that it was useless to carry on the discussion. Reading between the lines, I have an idea of why it was officially burned down. There are a number of log cabins in the reserve that are reachable by car, and these the government maintains. These cabins are rented out to vacationers who want to spend some time in the wilderness, and for this they pay a rental fee to the Quebec Government. The cabin that was set on fire, being accessible only by water, was not a revenue producer. I can imagine some bureaucrat at a desk making the economically correct decision to reduce maintenance expenses by getting rid of it. This person probably never even saw the cabin. It is a shame that those to whom we entrust some of our most sacred natural treasures are not always up to the task.

CHAPTER FIVE
LOUIE'S TILT

SOMETIME IN THE SIXTIES, Canadian *Maclean's Magazine* conducted a survey to discover in which province lived the country's happiest people. Newfoundland, which includes Labrador, was found to be that province. The following year, the province's automobile licence plates began displaying the words *Newfoundland - Canada's Happy Province*. The glad tidings proudly appeared on the province's plates for a number of years. I am not sure when the idea was dropped, but of one thing I am certain: it was not because the people were no longer happy. In 1999, I canoed in Labrador and can confirm that not only are the people happy, they transfer that happy feeling to outsiders they meet. Let me explain what I mean, starting with a bit of contextual history.

In July 1903, two Americans from the New York City area went to Labrador with adventure in mind. One was Leonidas Hubbard, a writer for *Outing Magazine*, and the other, Dillon Wallace, was a New York lawyer. They both fancied the outdoors, but had had limited experience in wilderness areas. One of the least-explored areas in North America at that time was the interior of Labrador. The two men, accompanied by a Cree-Métis helper from the James Bay region, arrived by steamship near the village of Northwest River in Labrador, the jumping-off point for the expedition. From there, the trio set out to canoe and portage over nine hundred kilometres northwest through the wildest part of the continent, planning to emerge in Ungava Bay, where Inuit lived. They did not make it. Without realizing it, they had taken the wrong river. Hubbard died of starvation on the trail back.

Those sad events of 1903 had long intrigued me. In 1999, my friend Phil Schubert and I decided to canoe the section of the expedition in which the fatal error occurred, paddling our canoe over the same route the Americans had followed to try to understand why they made the horrible mistake of going up the wrong river.

It was in this context that Phil and I arrived in Northwest River, Labrador in August 1999 after driving with a canoe on top of his van some two thousand kilometres from Ottawa, much of it on a gravel-bush road through Quebec and Labrador wilderness. We knew no one in the town, so we headed for the one place we had learned of before leaving on our trip: a modest museum in the old Hudson's Bay Company building with a small exhibit of Hubbard and Wallace artefacts in one room. We asked the young lad who was minding the museum at the time if he could put us on to someone who was familiar with the Hubbard and Wallace expedition. The boy offered that his father could probably help us. This information turned out to be a wonderful stroke of luck for us.

We headed for the house of Louie Montague, the lad's father, and met a short and obviously strong man whose aboriginal ancestry showed in his features and dark skin. Louie told us he was part Inuit. He got out his maps and pointed out a number of significant aspects of the trip we would be undertaking, giving us advice that we noted carefully. Then he made an astonishing offer, considering that he had only known us strangers from the city for the last half hour. He went into his bedroom and came back with a key in his hand. This was our second stroke of luck. "If you are going into that area, you can use my tilt," he said, and he handed us a key. A tilt, we knew, is a small log cabin that Labrador trappers use on their trapping rounds in the wintertime. They are built small, which makes them easy on firewood in the depths of the bitter-cold Labrador winters. Since a tilt is not very high, its door has to be correspondingly low, about one metre high in this case. This fact was not lost on my friend Phil, who is two metres tall. We were amazed at Louie's generosity.

Friend Michèle Paquette at Louie Montague's tilt on the Nascaupi River in Labrador, 2000.

Armed with Louie's key we paddled away from Northwest River at four o'clock that afternoon and made about six and a half kilometres up Grand Lake to a rounded point of land, behind which we slipped just so we could camp away from the village our first night. The following days we had to paddle a total of sixty-five kilometres northwest on Grand Lake and then twenty-five kilometres north on the Nascaupi River before reaching Louie's tilt, where we set up camp. We were lucky: high winds on Grand Lake had kept us wind-bound for only an afternoon. It is not always so easy on such a big lake.

Louie's tilt, which was on the large side for a tilt, held everything we could have wanted and more: two comfortable bunks, a table, chairs, a wood-burning stove with firewood, and everything else needed to be very, very comfortable in the middle of the Labrador wilderness. The tilt was sitting on top of a promontory overlooking the Nascaupi River at its confluence with the smaller Red Wine River, a water course we wanted to explore. The structure was solid, even though it had been built many years previously. Louie kept the logs dry with a preservative on the outside, and clean with varnish on the inside. A small window let light in through the front wall and another was set into the door. On the outside, a large splinter of wood had been gouged out of a corner post, leaving behind the deep, telltale imprint of a bear's claws that added wilderness authenticity to the structure. The cabin blended in perfectly with its surroundings and had become an integral part of the wilderness, almost as if it had grown there along with the trees. For Louie, this tilt was one of a series of four in a line he had built along his trapping route a long time ago, giving him a place to sleep every night he was on his trapline in the bitter Labrador cold. For us, it was a welcome haven for the three days we spent at the confluence of the two rivers.

On the first day following our arrival at the tilt, while exploring up the Red Wine River, we met two local hunters who were preparing their hunting camp in anticipation of the Canada goose season, for these people still lived very much on the fruits of the hunt. Their camp was higher up on the Nascaupi River. Two days later, we saw them again as they were coming back down the Nascaupi, heading for their homes in Northwest River. They stopped in to visit with us for a while, which we very much appreciated. It was an interesting coincidence that Lee Baikie worked for the telephone company and Val Rich for the power company, since my friend Phil is a power engineer and I am a telephone engineer.

When the time came for them to continue on home, they had a surprise for us. From their packs they took out some left over food they wouldn't be needing. First, out came a large Mason jar of preserved ptarmigan — the partridge of the north — followed by a huge jar of preserved moose meat, half a loaf of homemade bread, fresh butter, and some chocolate cookies. The next three days were the finest of our whole ten-day trip from the culinary point of view. What we had brought with us was mainly freeze-dried food, for the sake of lightness. It is not difficult to imagine the effect of this horn of plenty on our spirits.

In the succeeding days, Phil and I completed our work of trying to figure out what had caused the 1903 tragedy. One must be careful when looking at history and trying to interpret it. I think I was objective when, after evaluating our findings, I concluded that the lack of wilderness experience of the two Americans, and their refusal to rely on the knowledge of local aboriginal people, were most probably major causes of their deadly mistake. At least, that was my view of things. Phil didn't fully agree.

On the last two days of the trip back, we paddled down toward our original starting point the full seventy-kilometre length of Grand Lake from one end to the other through extremely calm and favourable conditions. The lake can whip up into very large waves, as we found out on the last day of our trip. Northwesterly winds can quickly come whistling down its length, whipping the water into an almost impassable barrier of waves, so we were lucky. We were lucky not to be faced with these conditions except for the very last hour of our trip.

Back in Northwest River and thinking about the unbelievable hospitality that Louie, Val, and Lee had offered us, we felt we had to respond in some way, though we could never compensate for all that we had received from these wonderful people. I am even a bit shy to say what it was that we did, but we really had no choice in such an out-of-the-way place. Phil and I each gave Louie a large case of beer, which we knew he would appreciate, and in the case of Val and Lee, they were at work and we could not see them, so we found out where their wives were and gave them each a large box of chocolates. It was they, after all, who had prepared the delicious food the two men had left with us.

Why is Newfoundland Canada's happy province? The sample size is small, but if our three benefactors are any indication of the norm, it's because of the extreme generosity of the people and their well-developed sense of sharing. How can these people not be happy if that is their way of life? Their happiness even rubs off on those who are fortunate enough to cross paths with them. Phil and I were very happy campers, indeed, living in Louie's tilt on the Nascaupi River for a few days, enjoying moose meat, ptarmigan, and home made bread.

Part Four

FARM YEARS

AT SOME TIME IN THE fifties, my forest-rambling friend Jacques Sauvé introduced me to Henry David Thoreau and *Walden*. This marvellous book quickly became my bible and changed my life. Thoreau became my hero and remains so to this day. Many of the thoughts that eventually led to his world-famous book were forged, hammered out, and massaged in the cabin that he built on the shore of Walden Pond. The effect of Thoreau's book, together with my own spiritual experiences in the wild cabins of my earlier life, combined to produce in me an irresistible urge to build my own cabin in the woods some day by the side of a wild lake. I knew I would, but I did not know where, and I did not know when. The next major shift in my lifestyle would be instrumental in achieving that dream, though I did not realize it at the time.

THAT FATEFUL SPRING

AFTER GRADUATING WITH A degree in electrical engineering from McGill University in Montreal, 1954, I married Constance, whom I had met in Shawinigan Falls as a summer student. The marriage lasted seventeen years, but unfortunately, we each grew in different directions and we eventually went different ways. I worked at a desk for the next twenty years, first in Montreal, then in Quebec City, and the final two years in Ottawa. During all those years, every moment I could spare from my professional and home life I spent in the great outdoors, most often somewhere in the province of Quebec, hiking or snowshoeing on wilderness trails, canoeing and fishing in isolated lakes and rivers, sleeping in tents or log cabins when possible. As the years advanced, I had more and more trouble reconciling the life I was living in large cities with the life that was most dear to me — the life my grandfather and my six uncles had introduced me to in my formative years: life in a rural environment where, just outside the door, the wilderness beckons.

The spring of 1974 is when I stopped trying to reconcile my two lives and took steps to make a drastic change in my lifestyle. I had met Elaine two years earlier and we were now living together as a couple in Ottawa.

Spring is a time of joyful renaissance — a time of primeval currents that surge and pulse in the human breast. At that time of the year, there is an increase in the number of cases where rationality gives way to impulsiveness that answers more to emotion than to cold reasoning. A bad case of this malady hit Elaine and me hard. Being out of doors became a priority, and we got the urge to make maple syrup. We both took a month off from work and started getting ready to tap. Neither of us had ever made syrup before.

The previous fall, while hiking the Gatineau Hills not far from our home in Ottawa, I had discovered an old, abandoned, one-horse stable in a grove of sugar maples. Though its planks were grey with age, its walls were still sound and the roof was tight. The stable had probably sheltered a workhorse decades ago in the days of the manual woodcutters. Neither the stable nor the surrounding forest showed any sign of recent human activity. We tried to find the owners of the land and its stable, but we weren't successful. The stable was ideal to house a small homemade evaporator. Finally, we decided to take a chance and go ahead with our plan to make syrup, and if the owners of the land and stable were to show up, we would share the syrup with them. If they wanted us to leave, we would, giving them the syrup we had made in thanks for the use of their land. As it turned out, the owners never came by and we never found out who they were.

The first thing we needed was an evaporator. While driving in downtown Ottawa one day, I spotted a forty-five-gallon steel drum set out for the garbage collectors. It was clean and had apparently been used for a bulk shipment of makeup, according to lettering on its side. I tied the drum onto the roof rack of my VW Beetle and took it home. Next, we bought two large, disposable, aluminum turkey-roasting pans from the supermarket to serve as the evaporator pans. With a small sledge and an axe as a can opener, I sliced two oval holes in the top of the drum to receive the pans, and a smaller, round hole in which to fit a length of stovepipe. Using the same technique, I cut a rectangular hole in the side of the drum for feeding in wood and fitted it with a curved, sheet-aluminum door on hinges. The abundant standing dead wood in the bush was just what we needed for fuel to boil down the sap.

We brought the evaporator to the stable and connected up its stove-pipe, which we ran carefully through a small window in the wall of stable, making sure there was sufficient clearance between the wood of the stable and the chimney. Next, we examined the trees that were not too far from the sugar shack, selected twenty-five of the larger, healthy sugar maples, and tapped them with a brace and bit. Into each hole we drove a spile with a hook on it and hung the buckets and covers. We were ready to make syrup.

But the temperature remained cold and the buckets stayed dry. A few days later, though, weather conditions turned ideal, freezing at night, sunny and warm in the daytime, and no wind. The buckets started filling up. We didn't need a storage tank, since the number of tapped trees was so small. We did the rounds on snowshoes at first, and then on foot as the snow melted, emptying the buckets directly into the evaporator pans. Our technique was a batch process rather than a continuous one as used in commercial operations. Whenever a pan filled up with boiling syrup at the proper temperature on a thermometer — 219° F (103.9° C) — we funnelled the golden liquid through a filter and into wine bottles, starting up again with a pan of fresh sap.

Elaine tending the homemade maple syrup evaporator, 1974.

Those were glorious days, and friends came out with us to take part in that most Canadian of spring rituals. One person brought a guitar, another a bottle of wine, and we sang folk songs in the sunshine and maple-scented air.

The weather remained good for syrup making during the whole month we had taken off from work. On our final day of vacation, we took apart our evaporator, removed the buckets, covers, and spiles from the trees, packed everything, including the syrup, in our VW Beetle, and drove home with the forty-five-gallon drum strapped to the top, leaving everything in the maple grove just as we had found it, minus a few dead trees we had used for fuel. The next day we went back to work in our respective offices.

Working in the warm spring sun, breathing the magic vapour of boiling syrup for a month, we had tasted pure paradise. Life had been very good. What we didn't realize at the time was that we had become intoxicated — intoxicated to the point that, in the days that followed our return to work, Elaine and I made a decision. We decided to quit our jobs and buy a farm not far from Ottawa — a farm that had a sugar bush with a functional sugar shack and all the equipment we needed to make maple syrup on a small, but commercial basis.

CHAPTER TWO

BUYING A FARM
AND SETTLING IN

If we listened to our intellect, we'd never have a love
affair. We'd never have a friendship. We'd never go into
business, because we'd be cynical. Well, that's nonsense.
You've got to jump off cliffs all the time and build your
wings on the way down.

— Ray Bradbury

IN 1974 ELAINE AND I DID exactly what Ray Bradbury had suggested:
we jumped off a cliff. If the decision was impulsive, the implementation
was more deliberate, but we were still jumping off a cliff. From May on
into summer we looked for a farm with a working sugar bush. There
were two major prerequisites: we had to be able to afford it, and it had
to be within feasible commuting distance from Ottawa. We had decided
that Elaine would quit her government job as soon as we bought a farm
to start in on the many tasks that were needed to turn the farm into
our home. I would pitch in on weekends and evenings, but during the
week I would continue working with the Bell Canada family for two
years to ease the transition to "voluntary poverty," as we referred to it.

Someone called us *les nouveaux pauvres* — like *les nouveaux riches*, only in the opposite direction. And, of course, the farm had to have a large, well-equipped sugar bush. We decided to look in the area of the Valley of the Little Nation, which I knew to be prime maple syrup country.

Friends suggested an approach for finding the farm we wanted and their method worked beautifully. We rattled around the dirt roads of the valley in our VW Beetle until we saw a neatly kept farmhouse with a sugar shack at the base of the mountain that rose behind the house. Our knocking at the farmhouse door summoned a grizzled old farmer. After complimenting him on the neatness of his farm, we asked if it happened to be for sale. He said it wasn't, but that didn't surprise us; we were expecting him to say that. The next question was our real reason for stopping: "Do you know of any nice farms for sale in this area that also have a sugar bush?" If farms are for sale in an area, the local farmers know about it.

The farmer suggested that we try about five miles down the road where there was an old farm for sale that had a sugar shack. We rattled on over to see the place, but the sugar bush was too small for our purposes. Still, the owner of that farm knew of another place, and so one old farm led to another.

Over several weekends, we followed up leads from farm to farm until late one afternoon we found the one that would be our home for the next ten years. It was being sold by the son of its previous owner, who had become too old to farm anymore. The land covered a hundred acres of low-rolling hill, twenty-five acres long and four acres wide, half of which was hayfield and half mature sugar-maple forest. The home was a small and quaint two-storey, squared-log house, over a hundred years old, situated on the road from Ottawa. The road, which was still gravel at the time, cut across the narrow dimension of the land. A third of the farm's acreage was in front of the house and two thirds were behind. In back of the house were two sheds — one for farm implements and the other a wood-storage shed and workshop — a chicken coop, and a large, cedar-shingled wooden barn built partly of logs and partly of planks.

The farm was situated at a T-intersection with another gravel road that ran in the long dimension of the property, toward the back of it, and farther up into a mountainous area. One thousand feet from the farm house along that road was the sugar shack. It was equipped for thirteen hundred taps and had a good, large evaporator. The operation was in three buildings: the sugar shack itself, where the syrup was boiled off; an old chicken coop a few metres away converted into what was called the "dining hall" for serving sugar-shack meals to paying guests; and a "dance hall" close by, to which the diners retired to work off their heaping meals by dancing to lively tunes squeezed out on an accordion by a local citizen. All this in the middle of a maple forest with a small stream flowing by. If we bought it, we were not only going to be in the business of making maple syrup; we would also be cooking up traditional sugar-shack meals for hungry visitors.

The farm met our two crucial requirements: it was just within reasonable temporary commuting distance from my job for the two years I would be working, and we could afford the price ... just barely. We bought it.

Well-meaning friends warned us that we would starve, we would go broke. "Have you made a budget?" we were asked. We had become intoxicated during that spring month of maple-syrup making and we were beyond being swayed by such rational approaches. We realized later that we were jumping off one of Ray Bradbury's cliffs, but there was no turning back. These same friends helped us move from Ottawa in early September, convinced that we were crazy. It even passed through our own minds that maybe we were.

In *Reflections from the North Country*, Sigurd Olson recalled words of counsel for a young man who had come to him for advice on taking a risk. "If you really want to do it, if it means that much to you, there is no choice but to go ahead." He told the man if he did not accept the risk, he would regret it the rest of his life. "You cannot turn your back on any challenge, physical or mental. If you do, you diminish yourself, and the next time it will be easier to say, 'No, I cannot do it.' If you take the hazards as they come and survive, you will be stronger and better and the trip will be a milestone in your life, one you will always know as a turning point."

Had we been able to read these words in 1974 before the move, they most certainly would have comforted us and helped convince us that perhaps we were not crazy.

On a late summer day in early September of 1974, Elaine and I mobilized our friends to help us move. We rented a truck, cooked up large pots of chilli, got a few cases of beer, and made a holiday of the move. That night, when everyone had left, Elaine and I collapsed onto the iron-and-brass bed that came with the farmhouse and slept like the proverbial logs, waking up to a beautiful and warm sunny day, ready to face our new life.

Time seemed to have stood still in the Valley of the Little Nation. It was as if the rest of the world had forgotten it existed. All roads in our area were gravel. Some farmers still used horses to work their farms and gather maple sap in the spring. Spinning wheels and hand looms were still used by women to make homespun yarn and to weave material for clothes. The men still made cedar shingles and shakes by splitting them with a tool called a "froe," which was driven by blows from a wooden club. We visited these farmers and saw that their tool sheds housed special handmade wooden benches for holding the split cedar pieces in place with the pressure of their feet while they planed them into shingles and shakes with a drawknife. Maple sap was still collected in buckets hung on trees. The tube system for collecting sap had yet to make serious inroads in the family farms of the Little Nation Valley.

We explored the sugar-bush trails that were used for gathering maple sap in the forested areas. They were great for hiking in the fall of the year. I also went farther afield, hiking up a dirt track that branched off the gravel road the sugar shack was on. The track headed up a steep peak called the Black Mountain. This was unknown territory for me, but I had a 1:50,000 scale topographic map of the area and, with the help of a compass, I could see where I was going.

About five kilometres up this track, the map showed a small lake a kilometre off in the bush. Taking a compass bearing on the lake, I pushed off into the forest, which quickly became hilly, rough, and rocky. Approaching the area where the lake should be, I kept my eyes peeled and, sure enough, ahead of me there was the blue reflection of water filtering through the leaves. The lake was oblong, about thirteen hundred feet long and four hundred wide. I followed the shore along the long side of the lake to about the middle, and there found a convenient rock at the water's edge from which one could dive into the deep. I took off my clothes and plunged in. The water was clear, cold, and refreshing after bushwhacking through the forest. The lake was completely wild with nary a building of any kind on its shores, and no road leading to it. I couldn't wait to get back to the farmhouse to share the news with Elaine. The next day, I took her there. "What a jewel you've found," Elaine exclaimed when she saw it.

Several times that fall, we hiked to the lake for a swim. It was not necessary to bring bathing suits. There was never a soul there. We even camped there with our dog one night under the stars, no tent. "I wonder who it belongs to?" I mused as we lay in our sleeping bags. "Perhaps we could buy a lot along the shoreline to build a cabin on." And that's where we left things for the time being.

Our first winter went by quickly. There were so many things to do to whip the farm into the shape we wanted. The previous owners had grown too old to properly keep up with all the repairs and general maintenance an old farm needs. In sprucing up the farmhouse as well as the other farm buildings, we had to develop new skills that we never thought were in us: plumbing, carpentry, electrical installations, building modifications, and general handy work. These were skills born of necessity. We could not afford to hire skilled labour to do all the repairs and maintenance. These skills were not innate in us, and we were surely nowhere as efficient as professionals, but develop them we did to the best of our ability.

That first year we didn't have animals for meat, nor did I cut our own firewood. We bought our meat and vegetables from local farmers and bought firewood for the kitchen stove from them, too. The main part of the house was heated by an oil-fired space heater, but this would change to wood heat the following year. We bought two calves in the spring, one a bull to be butchered the following fall when it had grown into a baby beef, and the other, a heifer, to produce calves for meat on a continuing basis. Chickens, ducks, and rabbits were added as sources of eggs and meat. We bought two freezers to hold all our meat as well as the vegetables from a quarter-acre garden. From the second year on, I cut all the firewood we needed to fuel not only the kitchen stove, but also an airtight Ashley wood-burning stove I installed in the central part of the house. The oil-burning space heater was stored in the shed.

Our water came from a spring some nine hundred feet away at the base of Black Mountain and flowed out of the faucets in the house and barn under the pressure of gravity. We felt secure in that we could be quite independent of commercially provided electricity in case of extended power failures, even in the depth of winter. The only things that absolutely needed electricity were the two freezers, and to protect them in case of a long power failure, we bought a gasoline-fuelled generator. We never had to use the generator in our ten years on the farm, but at least we slept more peacefully.

One morning, the cold-water tap in the bathroom seemed to be plugged. Not a drop came out of it. I was still working in Ottawa at this stage and was on the point of jumping into the car for the daily drive to Ottawa. Not wanting to leave Elaine without water in the bathroom for the day, I decided to have a quick look to try and solve the problem before leaving. I closed the valve that controlled the flow to that faucet and screwed the top of it off. There was a foreign object sticking out of the faucet opening. I pulled on it and out came the hind leg of a frog. I quickly disposed of the severed leg before Elaine could see it, screwed the faucet back together, turned the water back on, and the flow of water was restored. I was pretty sure I knew how the frog got in. Nine hundred feet up the pipe to where the spring flows out of the mountain rock is a concrete basin in which is submerged the upper end of the pipe. I guessed that the screen over the end of the pipe was gone, or rusted through, but I didn't have time to check that out right then. There was no way I was going to tell Elaine about the frog's leg and then say, "Goodbye, I'm off to work," so I just said, "You have water now. Goodbye, I'm off to work." I never did tell her the nature of the problem until years later.

The question readers probably have in their minds right now is no doubt the same one that popped into my head at the time: What happened to the rest of the frog? Well, I am sorry to disappoint you, but that's a mystery I wasn't able to figure out. Never again, though, did frog parts appear in our water supply after a new screen was placed over the input end of the water pipe at the foot of the mountain.

That first winter we discovered that the long dirt track winding up Black Mountain toward the small lake we had discovered was a natural ski trail. On mornings when a heavy, overnight fall of snow greeted our awakening, we put all work aside, ate breakfast, and headed out the back door on our cross-country skis. We had learned that the uphill, gravel road leading to the track up the mountain would not be ploughed before noon, so we set off up the road on our skis through the magical powder snow for a kilometre, and then turned left onto the track that led upward toward the lake. The first part of the track climbed steeply and long, three kilometres up the mountain to a peak that overlooked the valleys below as far as the eye could see. The deep, powdery snow and the right wax gave us a good grip for our skis in climbing the steep track. After herring-boning for an hour from the farmhouse up the dirt road and then the track, we reached the summit, puffing and sweating like stevedores. Later, we counted the contours on a topographic map and found that we had climbed three hundred metres above the elevation of the farm. Way off in the distance we could see another mountain peak at about our level, or maybe even a bit higher, with wavy white lines on its flanks snaking their way down from the top. We were peering at Mont Tremblant Ski Centre, which I later measured on a map to be some seventy kilometres distant.

After recovering our breath and enjoying the view for some minutes, Elaine and I turned and peered back down the hill we had climbed, looked into each other's eyes for a few seconds. I nodded to her, and down she went, with me following. We schussed all the way down the mountainside, needing little effort to slow us down because of the deep powder. It was an exhilarating run with flying skis on the edge of wipeout, down three kilometres to where the mountain track turned right onto the still-unploughed gravel road, down the hill for another kilometre of fast running, finally turning sharp right into our own backyard, skidding to a powdery stop at the farmhouse, where we fell into each other's arms, completely out of breath and laughing like a pair of loons. Skiing had rarely been better. Paraphrasing Sigurd Olson again, perhaps we'd had more fun before, but we couldn't remember where.

CHAPTER THREE

THE FIRST YEARS ON THE FARM

IN THE SPRING OF 1975, we tapped our sugar bush and made syrup on a modestly commercial basis for the first time in our lives. We were lucky to have the help of the previous owner's son, Gilles, for the syrup part of the operation, and his wife, Marcelle, for preparing the sugaring-off meals of pork and beans, soufflé omelette, fried pork rind, eggs poached in syrup, and maple taffy poured on the snow.

It was essential that Gilles and Marcelle be there to help Elaine and me ease into our new roles of "restaurant" operator and syrup maker respectively, two new items to add to our growing list of compulsory skills needed to survive in our venture. Gilles shared with me his vast store of knowledge gained from many years of experience making syrup first with his parents, and later on his own. He showed me all kinds of syrup makers' tricks, such as preventing the evaporator pan from boiling over, which it has a tendency to do, by waving a popsicle stick slathered with butter over the bubbling pan. As if by magic, the bubbles immediately drop back down into the pan, and a crisis is averted. It was really a dramatic show for the uninitiated, which we were at that time. I found out later that it is a trick spaghetti cooks use to keep the pasta pot from boiling over, but I

Elaine collecting sap
with daughter Amanda
watching, 1977.

had never heard of this before. The technical explanation is that just a few drops of oil from the melting butter is all that is needed to destroy the surface tension of the threatening bubbles and they simply all burst and the pan settles down.

There was one skill that Gilles had never mastered, though, and that was making golden bricks of maple sugar. When I asked him to show me how to make sugar one day, he quickly admitted his ignorance of this folk art, but suggested I see Émilien St-Pierre in the village, a really old sugar maker. It turned out to truly be an art, and not a science, at least how Émilien did it.

One day, when the sap wasn't running and I had some free time, I brought two gallons of my syrup over to Émilien's house in the village for a lesson. In his kitchen, Émilien had an old-fashioned, wood-burning cookstove with round iron lids that fit into a rectangular iron panel over the firebox. He took away all this ironwork, which meant that the top of the firebox was just a big, open hole. Over this, Émilien set a special

Left: A hired hand collecting sap with the farm tractor, 1977.

Below: Young friend Jeremy working on a big maple, 1978.

Courtesy of Douglas Ward.

stainless-steel pan that fit neatly over the open firebox, and directed me to pour in the syrup, which I did. Émilien went into the shed just off his kitchen to get some small, dry spruce and cedar sticks. He stuffed the firebox with crumpled newspaper, laid down a few sticks of wood, struck a match, and soon had a blaze going.

The way to make maple sugar from syrup, according to Émilien, was to boil off the right amount of moisture, let the thickened syrup cool some, beat it with a wooden paddle until it started to crystallize, and then, at exactly the right moment, pour it into moulds to harden into golden bricks. The whole process seemed pretty straightforward except for one very critical step: determining when the syrup had boiled enough. Not enough, and the sugar will not harden, but will remain semi-liquid; too much, and the sugar bricks take on the hardness of building bricks.

Émilien's hot fire soon had the syrup boiling.

After what seemed to me to be a long time, I became impatient and asked, "Is it ready?"

"Not yet," answered Émilien. He was a man of few words.

A few minutes later, "Soon?" I asked hopefully.

"Soon," repeated Émilien without turning his eyes away from the steaming pan.

"How will you know when it's ready?" I asked with anxious eagerness.

"Don't be so impatient," admonished Émilien. "You city people have no patience." I couldn't argue with that. "Just a few more minutes."

Émilien stirred some more, examined the syrup dripping from his spoon, then continued stirring. I could sense a quickening of his movements. "Soon, very soon now." Émilien was obviously getting excited. More stirring, more examination of dripping syrup, and then suddenly he straightened up and announced, "I think it's ready now."

He quickly raised his free hand to his mouth and, in one deft movement, removed his false teeth. "My God", I thought, "how do his teeth fit into this process?" With his other hand, he raised a spoonful of hot syrup to his pursed lips and blew a short, explosive breath of air across the level top of the spoon. "Poof!" I watched in awe as a big golden bubble of syrup went floating off gently on a current of steam rising from the boiling pan. He shoved his teeth back into the safety of his mouth, announcing with a big, toothy, and self-satisfied grin, "It's ready!"

Émilien and I lifted the heavy pan off the stove, set it down on a wooden table, and began beating the cooling syrup with wooden paddles until it crystallized. Then we poured the solidifying sugar into the moulds and let it cool further. The golden bricks of sugar had just the right hardness and consistency. The syrup had indeed been ready, and Émilien's teeth were safely back where they belonged.

The claim to local fame of Gilles' wife Marcelle in this operation was her soufflé omelettes, which, through her culinary skills, she managed to make rise three or four inches. Guests told us they came to our sugar shack especially for Marcelle's omelettes. Indeed, they were heavenly, and her pork and beans were special, too. She prepared all her secret ingredients the evening before a sugar-shack party and put them together with the beans in large, covered, black iron pots. Gilles took the pots over to the village baker, who carefully slid them into his large, hot, wood-fired oven on a maple paddle after he finished baking his bread for the day, and left them in there all night in the very slowly cooling oven. The next morning the oven was still quite hot and by lunchtime the beans were cooked to perfection. The smells that came from the bean pots were heavenly.

People started arriving around eleven o'clock, and some wanted taffy on the snow *before* they sat down to a truly filling meal of beans, omelette, eggs poached in syrup, pork rinds, and all kinds of pickles and other condiments. This I could never understand: sweet taffy before a heavy meal? After, yes, but before? Different strokes for different folks. I quit trying to understand.

One Good Friday, a stout chap arrived at the sugar shack and asked me to serve him a dozen eggs poached in syrup.

"Twelve eggs poached in syrup?"

"Yes, twelve eggs."

"For you?"

"Yes for me."

"Okay."

I gave him his twelve poached eggs and he ate them all as I watched to see if he would really finish them off. He did, although he slowed down some near the end. I found out later that he was the owner of a steakhouse in the nearby village of Chénéville, which was open 364 days a year, but not on Good Friday. On that day each year, he and his family came to our sugar shack for his traditional spring meal.

A few months after the twelve-eggs episode, Elaine and I went to Chénéville for a steak supper at his restaurant. I told the waitress I wanted to order twelve steaks.

"Twelve steaks? To take with you?" she asked.

"No. To eat here."

"To eat here?" she questioned with a raised eyebrow.

"Yes, to eat here."

"Just a minute."

And off she went in a huff to get the owner. Out he came from the kitchen with a "What are you, a troublemaker?" attitude about him.

"What's this about twelve steaks?" he asked, arms akimbo.

"Well," I said calmly, "you had twelve poached eggs in syrup at my sugar shack, why can't I have twelve steaks at your restaurant?"

For a second he was stunned, but then his face lit up as he remembered the eggs, and, realizing we were pulling his leg, he burst out laughing.

"Those last ones were really pretty hard to get down. I didn't think I was going to make it," he confessed. "But I couldn't quit. I would have lost face."

Elaine and I sat down to delicious filet mignons — only one apiece, though — accompanied by a good red wine and followed by a digestive on the house.

After their meals in the "dining hall," people retired to the "dance hall" for lively folk dances and polkas to the tune of a swaying accordion, vigorously pumped by a stomping, sweating villager. Here, our replete guests worked off the heavy calories of their sugar-shack meals with the exuberance typical of French Canadians having fun.

From the beginning of our first season, Gilles had always been in charge of firing and operating the evaporator. It was no simple task and there are many potential pitfalls that could easily ruin the syrup, and even the expensive evaporator pans. It was extremely important to ensure a continuous flow of sap to the four large evaporator pans sitting atop the raging inferno in the firebox. Problems could range from running out of sap in the main holding tank just outside the sugar shack, to a broken or plugged coupling pipe between pans. If one of these problems occurred, immediate action was required to cut the draft by opening the firebox doors and somehow keeping liquid in the pans, be it with buckets of sap, or even water and, in the extreme, even shovelfuls of snow, until the fire died down. At best, a whole batch of syrup and valuable time would be lost. At worst, the evaporator pans would be scorched and had to be replaced. This could mean not only a major expenditure, but would also put an end to the syrup season for that year. New pans would have to be ordered and manufactured for the following season. At the extreme worst, the scorching syrup could catch fire — it is quite flammable — and burn the sugar shack to the ground.

A couple of weeks into the season, after watching and helping Gilles, I felt I was ready to boil off syrup by myself. When the steaming pans were cooling down at the end of the day's boiling one afternoon, I told Gilles how I felt and that I wanted to start up and operate the evaporator the following morning — alone. I could tell from Gilles' body language that he was not entirely comfortable with the idea. I persisted. After all, it was now my sugar shack, although I could understand Gilles' emotions about putting his "baby" into the hands of a rank amateur. I am sure he had visions of all the disaster scenarios described above. He finally gave in, though, and the following morning I was on my own. Gilles' parting words were an anxious-sounding, "*Manque pas ta chotte!*" — Don't miss your shot!

The new responsibility I had given myself did not weigh lightly on my shoulders. I was very conscious of the disastrous consequences of a misstep on my part. The only person around to solve any problems that might arise was going to be me. Was there enough sap in the outside holding tank? Check. Was the connection between the holding tank and the first big pan in order? Check. Was the float valve at the entrance to the first pan free? Check. This valve was crucial because it controlled the level of sap in the pans. Were the three connecting pipes between the four pans free of leaks and plugs? Check. It was time to fire up.

I swung open the heavy cast-iron doors of the cavernous firebox, stuffed in newspapers and small starter sticks, and struck a match. As the fire caught, I piled in three-foot lengths of softwood sawmill slab. The roaring of the draft was surprisingly loud. Softwood slab burns quickly and hot, which is what is needed for good syrup making. The appetite of that firebox was monstrous. Between feeding the fire, constantly checking all pipes and connections, verifying sap level in the pans, and carefully

Feeding slab into
the firebox of the
commercial-sized
maple-syrup evaporator
on the farm, 1975.

watching the thermometer in the very front pan ——— which is where
the sap finally turns into syrup at 219°F — I did not have much time to
daydream. The real peak of activity occurred when I was doing all those
things and, at the same time, the thermometer finally registered 219°F. At
that temperature, the syrup was ready. I had to immediately pour it off,
filter, and can or bottle it while it was still boiling hot to ensure sterility
in the containers — and perform all the other tasks as well.

That first day on my own was a draining one, both physically and
mentally, but that night when I shut down, I felt the wonderful satisfaction
of having won my stripes. After a few more sessions of tending the roaring
syrup machine by myself, I became comfortable with the job, even though
I felt a bit like an old-time railway fireman feeding cords of wood nonstop
into the flaming maw of a locomotive's firebox to keep the train running
on time.

One day I had a good laugh. Kneeling on the cement floor in front of
the open firebox doors, I was stuffing in slab after slab of tinder-dry pine,
spruce, and fir when I happened to glance behind me through the open
door of the sugar shack. There, on the gravel road that passed by, was a

tourist, also on bended knee, with a camera to his eye taking a snapshot of a local peasant out of a quaint scene from the past: me. As soon as he saw me looking at him, he immediately clicked his camera, then took off at a run back to his car and drove off without a word. I felt that I had truly arrived as a quaint *nouveau pauvre*.

⁂

After a good day's run of sap, I would often boil late into the night to ensure that there was enough room left in the collecting tank for the following day's run. Good weather for heavy sap runs is a combination of warm, sunny days and below-freezing temperatures at night. The night sky is usually clear under these conditions. Boiling off alone at night with a pitch-black sky overhead pierced by sparkling points of celestial fire and crackling frost underfoot was awe-inspiring. Warmth was, of course, not a problem inside the sugar shack, and in fact it was refreshing to step outside once in while to cool off. Looking up into the black sky, I could see that the evaporator chimney was adding its own hot, orange-coloured shooting stars to the black, velvet dome overhead. The sparkling vault seemed immense and I felt like such a small thing in that immensity, which in fact I was.

Shutting down the evaporator took the better part of an hour. I had to be sure that the heat remaining in its slowly cooling iron body would not dry out and scorch the evaporator pans.

When all was properly shut down, I turned off the one light, closed the sugar-shack doors, and walked unhurriedly the thousand feet down to the darkened farmhouse below on the crisp, freezing, gravel road, craning my neck upwards, marvelling at the constellations twinkling in a sky as black as it can get only in the country in winter. That leisurely end-of-the-day walk in the crackling, frosty darkness was sheer pleasure.

Elaine had long ago gone to bed. I did a quick wash to remove the stickiness and major areas of dirt before crawling into a bed kept warm by my sleeping wife. I felt so comfortable and satisfied, and immediately fell into the deep sleep that is the reward of a long day of good, hard, honest labour.

We continued making syrup for the next eight years, but for only one more season did we continue serving sugar-shack meals. We found that it required far too much trouble and outlay of funds for what it brought in, and the party atmosphere that accompanied this part of the operation was not really what we had come to the country for. What we really enjoyed was collecting the sap and making the syrup, not so much the crowds.

∞

In the spring of 1975, we found out that the land around the lake on the mountain was owned by an elderly woman from a nearby village who could no longer take care of her affairs, so her brother, a priest, looked after them for her. We also found out that the lake was called Lac des Vieux Mon-Oncles — Lake of the Old Uncles — by some previous owners whose ancestors had inherited the lake years ago from their old uncles. When we cast our lines into it we discovered that the lake harboured large fish: small-mouth bass of two and three pounds. The upshot of our negotiations was that in the fall, the priest, not wanting to make a large profit in selling the land surrounding the lake, which would have bothered his conscience as well as his sister's, sold it to us for an unbelievably low price. Not just a lot on the lake, but the whole lake and the three hundred acres of land surrounding it. Our joy knew no bounds. Now I knew where one day I would build the log cabin my soul craved.

∞

In March of 1976 a new magazine made its appearance on the Canadian publishing scene and took off like a rocket. It was called *Harrowsmith*, and it especially targeted people with city backgrounds who wanted to be part of the "back to the land" movement of the seventies. Well, Elaine and I had spent all our adult lives studying and working in cities and here we were "on the land," so we surely qualified as targets for *Harrowsmith*. I felt that the magazine fit in very well with our needs, for we still had a lot to learn. I also felt, though, that I had something to offer the readers of the publication, and so I wrote an article on wild mushrooms, a subject I am familiar with, and together with a dozen slides I had taken, sent it in to *Harrowsmith*. Receiving the letter of acceptance was a real thrill.

The article appeared in the sixth issue of the publication in March 1977, and started a very satisfying long-term relationship with the magazine, during which I wrote articles for them on a regular basis. I was particularly pleased one day when I was introduced to some visitors from

France who were visiting our sugar shack and one young lady exclaimed in French, "Ah Monsieur Kenney, you write for 'arrowsmit, is it not?" The magazine had become enormously popular with back-to-the-landers not only in Canada, but in the United States and in many other countries of the world.

It was during this period that I realized how important it was to have a peaceful mind if I wanted my writing to be worthwhile. If I had a subject about which I felt passionate and my mind was at ease, I found that I could write in a way that pleased not only me, but others as well. I also found out that if either the passion or the peace of mind were absent, there was no use trying to write. If peace of mind is important for writing, then surely it must also be important for many other aspects of our lives that affect our long-term wellbeing. Looking for peace of mind was a major driving force that had motivated us to quit our jobs in the city in the first place and move to the country.

On the day I finally quit my job in the city almost two years after moving to the farm, July 14, 1976, our first daughter was born. We called her Amanda, which was my grandmother's name. Our daughter also shared her great grandmother's birth date, which is just one day before mine. Amanda became Mandy for family and friends. This event added a whole new dimension to our reality. Life was good. Peace of mind that I feel is necessary to nurture creativity settled in on a long-term basis.

✎

In the summer of 1976, I decided to become a beekeeper, something I knew nothing about. I bought two classic books to learn about this new initiative that would add to our income: *ABC and XYZ of Bee Culture* by A.I. Root, and *The Hive and the Honey Bee*, edited by Dadent and Sons. With the help of these books, and the advice of a Department of Agriculture bee expert, another back-to-the-lander and I each built two beehives and filled them with bees the following spring. As unlikely as it seemed to us at first, it was possible to order boxes of bees to populate our hives and receive them through the mail. It was with a high degree of trepidation that I took delivery of my first two buzzing boxes of bees in the spring of 1977.

The boxes were open to the air on two sides except for stout screening that covered the openings. Inside were hordes of wriggling, buzzing bees sensing the great outdoors through the screening and — or so I thought at first — searching madly for a way to get out of the box. There was one special and very small screened box attached to the inside of each large box among the hundreds of milling bees. It was special because it held the queen bee, whose presence all the other bees could perceive while remaining physically isolated from her by screening. There has to be a getting-to-know-you period between a new queen and her subjects before she goes out among them, otherwise they may kill her. This small, separate box within the big box was part of that acclimatizing process.

The box of bees must then be "installed" in a hive. This step, when one has only read about it, is nerve-wracking in the extreme. Clad in head-veil and gloves, and armed with a smoker — a special contraption that produces clouds of smoke to pacify the bees — I gently opened one of the boxes of bees by removing its top wooden panel with the help of my hive tool — a special steel tool for working with hives. This opens the way for all the bees to escape, but I soon realized, with great relief, that they are not at all interested in doing that. The next step is to remove the small screened cage containing the queen bee and to put it aside. Actually, if the weather is cool, it is recommended to put the queen-bee cage in your pocket to keep her warm while you are installing the worker bees. This I did. Then I inverted the large box with the now-open top and shook it over the hive, and knocked it against the top of the bees' new home to induce the workers to drop into it. The stubborn ones are convinced to enter by knocking the box harder on the hive to dislodge them. The next step is critical and when I installed my first box of bees I completely forgot about it in my sweat to close off the hive with its cover and be done with the job. It was Elaine who was standing by at a respectable distance who brought me back to reality. "What about the one in the little box you put in your pocket?"

"Good Lord!" I cried, "The queen!" Without her, the hive is sterile.

With jittery nerves, I removed the cover of the hive, now full of bees, and took the queen cage from my pocket, carefully installed it between two honey frames inside the hive, and then closed the hive again. I breathed a huge sigh of relief. The queen cage has an ingenious escape-hatch arrangement that eventually allows her to escape her small cage and join her now-familiar subjects. The escape hatch is a hole plugged with a sweet substance that beekeepers call candy. The other bees eat this candy away over a period of a couple of days while getting used to their queen, and finally release her. Hopefully, she is accepted by them. She is their guarantee for the survival of the hive by virtue of her prodigious production of thousands of fertilized eggs, which she lays in hexagonal cells of beeswax. I installed the second box in its hive with much less nervousness and without forgetting the queen this time, but installing that first hive was hairy.

Eventually, over the next few years, I worked our apiary up to thirty hives, which made a significant contribution to our economic wellbeing. A hive produced somewhere from one to two hundred pounds of honey in an average year in our area. Assuming even a poor year, that meant at least some three thousand dollars of revenue added to our meagre income.

One day the phone rang and a heavily accented eastern European voice asked, "Mr. Kenney, I come see your bees, yes?" I told the caller that I would be working in the apiary that afternoon and gave him instructions on how to find me. At the appointed time, a car pulled up on the dirt road running near the hives; a heavy-set older man got out and walked into the apiary. He did not seem mindful of the bees that could sting him if he managed to accidentally apply physical pressure to one or more. I cautioned that he be more careful or he'd be stung. His next words told me why he had come, "That's what I want, that's what I want." He wanted to be stung, and I immediately knew why. "Do you mind?" he asked me. "No, I don't mind," I replied. With his left hand he carefully picked up a bee between thumb and forefinger, placed it on the back of his other hand and squeezed the bee, which provoked it to sting. "Oh," he moaned with a grimace of pain, "That feels good, that feels good," all the while rubbing his hands together. Then he changed hands and repeated the same procedure on the other hand, resulting in more moaning and hand-rubbing.

I glanced at his hands and saw what I expected to see: they were deformed by arthritis. Treatment of that joint disease with bee venom was once common practice in North America, even as recently as the first half of the twentieth century, and in Europe the practice carried on into the latter parts of the century as well and perhaps continues today. He explained to me that many doctors in his native Russia kept a hive or more of bees for the express purpose of treating arthritic patients. He marvelled that in Canada he could get treated for free, as most beekeepers would not begrudge him the loss of a bee or two. In Russia, he said, he had to pay a doctor a good sum of roubles to get stung. He never came back for further treatments, so I have concluded that the single treatment my bees administered to him cured him of his malady. At least, that is what I'd like to think.

⁓

We derived another benefit from our beehives thanks to Médard Lavergne, the local farrier who came to our farm once a year to check out and trim the hooves of our two large pinto ponies, which were big enough that Elaine and I could ride them as well as the girls. Médard was a powerfully built, good-humoured old farmer shaped like an iron-pumping Santa Claus and just as jolly. He was a great source of practical folklore for all kinds of things. Médard noticed our supply of honey supers, which are the rectangular wooden boxes with no top and no bottom that are piled up one on top of the other to form beehives. The supers themselves are hollow, and it is in them that frames of wax are hung for bees to deposit honey in. Each super is about ten inches high.

"Do you have any rhubarb?" the farrier asked.

"Yes" we replied. "Over there near the shed."

"Take one of those hollow honey boxes," as he called them, "and put it over a rhubarb plant when it is growing in the spring, and after a while put a second one on top of that. The plant will search for the sun and grow as long as your arm and thick as your wrist." We tried it and, indeed, got the longest and thickest rhubarb I have ever seen.

Médard's rhubarb trick worked as advertised, but some of the others he recommended to us were not as successful, largely because we didn't try them. For example, an open wound could be kept sterile, he suggested, by packing it with droppings from a black cow — not just any colour, mind you. The cow had to be black. We gave that one a pass and stuck to traditional medicine when necessary.

If we had had a cow in need of being dried after calving, I think we would have also passed up the next remedy offered by Médard. To dry a cow, he recommended filling a bucket full of red-hot coals, setting it under the cow's udder, and milking her into the sizzling, hot coals. I don't doubt that a poor cow subjected to that treatment would seriously tense her udder as tightly against her belly as she could, and milk would not be forthcoming for some time.

Médard's last recommendation that day had to do with *herbe à fièvre,* or "fever grass" — Blue verbena. Picked in the summer and hung up to dry, he used it as an herbal tea to ward off colds and grippes. Our friend Antoine, from the city, said that he used it for that purpose, too, and it worked for him, so it wasn't just a country custom anymore. Perhaps old Médard got in his yearly supply of verbena for another reason as well, which he didn't reveal to us. A well-known and highly respected scientific book from Quebec titled *Flore Laurentienne* ("Laurentian Flora"), written by Catholic brother Marie-Victorin, says about verbena, "[t]he generic name signifies Vein of Venus alluding to its supposed powers as an aphrodisiac." Well, the winter nights did tend to be severe and quite long in the dark depths of Quebec winters in the country. One had to be prepared.

CHAPTER FOUR

BUILDING THE CABIN

IN THE AUTUMN OF 1976, I started thinking seriously about building the long-desired log cabin on the shores of Lake of the Old Uncles. I was really starting from scratch here, never having done much building in my life. My research had uncovered three interesting books on cabin building: *The Wilderness Cabin* by Calvin Rutstrum, *How to Build and Furnish a Log Cabin* by W. Ben Hunt, and *Building with Logs* by B. Allan Mackie. Studying these books made me realize that we had several choices of design for the cabin, and that to settle on one particular design would take considerable thinking about the advantages and disadvantages of each. This would be a good winter project. We also realized that there were a few other critical questions to answer before even thinking of design. For example, where was the best place to locate the cabin and with what orientation? How big did we want it to be? And how much suitable space was there available on the shore of the lake to build it on?

Elaine and I decided that, to keep things simple, the cabin would have just one big room — no interior separating walls. We had to answer these questions before the snow flew if my winter studies were to be productive enough to start the physical work the following spring.

I walked around the shore of the lake several times, carefully examining and evaluating every possible building site before making a final decision, taking into account a number of factors: accessibility to the water; availability of bedrock outcroppings to act as a foundation for the bottom logs; orientation of the cabin (we wanted the front to face south); sufficient space for a reasonable-sized structure; and protection from the bitter, cold north wind in winter. In the end there was really only one possible site that met all these requirements.

One crucial factor was accessibility to the water for swimming. Although the lake is quite deep a certain distance away from shore, there was only one place around the lake's perimeter that permitted diving into deep water directly from shore. The lake has a muddy bottom near shore, as a lot of small mountain lakes do, and everywhere else but in this one place it would be necessary to step through soft mud to get to water deep enough for swimming, which is no fun. The location I settled on was about twenty-five feet wide along the shore, where a huge, rocky cliff plunges down from a great height toward the lake, but just before reaching it, levels off onto a small, rocky plateau for some fifty feet before again continuing its downward plunge into the water. From this small plateau, one can dive into deep water, swim to anywhere in the lake and back, and come out by walking up a smooth, rocky, underwater slope off to the side of the diving area, never having set foot in mud.

The rocky plateau was large enough to easily accommodate a good-sized, one-room cabin with a covered front porch. I would only have to cut down two medium-sized trees to clear out the space required. A cabin in this location would face south-by-twenty degrees west, which was close enough to due south for us. At three spots in the building area, bedrock emerged from the forest floor in just the right places to provide good, solid support for three corners of the cabin. For the one remaining corner, a posthole would have to be dug down below frost level to take a six-inch diameter cedar post that could be cut from the surrounding forest. Protection from the north wind was automatically guaranteed by the high, rocky cliff that rose at the back of the building site. The location was chosen and I was ready to start the design of the cabin.

The size and basic design of the cabin were influenced by two important factors: first, building it was to be a one-person project, with a bit of help from one or two other people when it came to setting the highest roof logs in place. And second, all the material that was not logs would have to be brought in by muscle power over a rough, one-kilometre footpath in the dense forest.

Over the winter, I read and re-read the three books on cabin building, made sketches, did calculations, and, after much thinking, finally decided on a structure fourteen feet wide and seventeen feet from front to back, inside dimensions. The front, fourteen-foot-wide wall with a door and a window in it would face the lake, and the rear one would back onto the rocky cliff behind. The seventeen-foot walls, one with a window in it, would form the two sides of the structure. A six-foot, covered porch in front would run the entire width of the cabin.

I chose saddle notches to lock the logs to each other at the corners. They are called saddle notches because they sit one on the other just like a saddle fits on a horse's back. The type of trees used to construct the cabin would be spruce and fir, which were the most abundant softwoods near the cabin site.

∽

Throughout the year, living on the farm, we experienced moments of great satisfaction that came from completing tasks at hand and then moving on to the next ones. Closing down the maple-syrup operation was one of those tasks that brought with it a feeling of great satisfaction when it was finished, leaving us with many gallons of syrup to sell during the coming year. We also ended up with syrup galore for ourselves, which we appreciated.

Getting in the year's firewood, putting up our fruit and vegetables, getting our chickens and other meat into the freezers, and, later on when we kept bees, getting our honey crop in, were all activities accompanied by a sense of closure and satisfaction. We had rarely found the same sense of completion and accomplishment when doing office work. Moving on from maple syrup to starting construction of the cabin in April 1977 was particularly satisfying that spring.

I have been asked how I found time to build the cabin with all the farm chores to be done. The type of farm we bought was a subsistence farm. It was not large and was far from occupying all our time. It took three years to build the cabin because I worked alone and was not at it for long periods at a time, but only worked at it when I could, here and there. Both Elaine and I worked at the farm chores and looked after the children, which included doing fun things in the woods and fields together, but Mom and Dad each had other things to do as well. Elaine made crafts and sold both hers and those of other farm women in a tiny shop that we built in one of the maple-syrup buildings. She also taught English to families who were not satisfied with the school system in Quebec at the time, and knew the importance not only of raising bilingual children, but of being bilingual themselves. Elaine also participated in the establishment of a *ludothèque*, which is the equivalent of a lending library, only for toys, not books. One day she bought a sulky and hitched up one of our ponies and showed up at the village five kilometres away to do her shopping. The local farmers were impressed, since very few of them still used horses.

Meanwhile, I was building a cabin, writing, and mobilizing the farmers to hack out a cross-country ski trail between the villages on either side of us. Building the cabin was really just a sideline, but a very, very important one, especially for me, although the whole family would use and enjoy it when it was finished.

Before starting construction, logs had to be cut. The spruce and fir trees needed were all on the other side of the lake. That meant choosing the trees closest to shore to avoid dragging them too far through the forest before sliding them into the lake. I would figure out later how to get them across. Realizing that I would be handling most of these logs myself, choice of trees was limited to eight inches maximum at the butt end (twelve-inch logs would have been far too heavy. The total number of logs needed to build the cabin was roughly eighty, and nine of the logs had to be twenty-five feet long. They were the ones that ran from the front of the porch to the back of the cabin — two at floor level to support the full weight of the cabin and seven to support the roof.

In the spring and summer of 1977, I managed to cut, peel, and toss into the lake fifty-eight logs, using a chainsaw to fell them and an axe to peel them. All except the four foundation logs would spend a year in the water until needed the following spring. The four foundation logs I swam individually across the lake and took out onto the large, flat rock on shore at the cabin site. My goal was to at least establish the base of the cabin before quitting for the year. When the time did come to quit because of oncoming winter weather, the four base logs were in place on their three foundation rocks and one post, and a bunch of logs still floated around at various points of the lake. A surprising number floated over close to the cabin site on their own, and I was able to pull them out of the water and drag them on shore that fall. The rest would have to be corralled in the spring.

What a marvellous gift to mankind are stands of spruce and fir. They provide ideal building material for wilderness construction that is in perfect harmony with the surroundings. In the spring, when the sap is up, peeling the bark from these trees is gratifying work. At one end of a log, a strip of the bark is separated with an axe from the wood of the trunk for three or four inches, and then a vigorous pull on the strip peels it off the tree for six, seven, or more feet like a huge banana peel. Once started, the rest of the bark comes off easily, revealing a glistening, healthy, attractive, almost white log underneath, ready for the log pile. The fragrance of the abundant sap is delightful and lingers on hands and clothes. It reminded me of the woodsy perfume emanating from lumberjacks drinking beer in my grandfather's inn after a hard day's work in the evergreen forest.

Building the cabin was physically demanding, but the wilderness surroundings were very pleasant and I could not have been happier. This was especially the case in the spring, when, resting between logs that I felled and peeled and when stopping for lunch, I was rewarded by the magic of birdsong echoing constantly in an amphitheatre of greenery. At times, different animals caught my attention. More than once, an inquisitive moose following a game path emerged from the forest in one corner of the lake to find out what manner of beast was disturbing the silence, only to seemingly melt back into the leaves and disappear, as quietly as it had arrived, no doubt having satisfied its curiosity. There was a beaver house on the lake near where the moose came out and spreading "V"s moving across the water's surface toward evening betrayed the presence of the residents, as did the occasional loud thwack of a tail slapping water. Sometimes on warm, sunny days, Elaine and I would pack a lunch and drive up the track to the beginning of the footpath through the forest. Carrying Amanda in our arms, we would walk the last kilometre to the cabin site and enjoy some hours of peace and quiet together while I did some light work on our project.

A friend commented that the project sounded like a lot of work. I won't deny that, but I did not work every day at it. I was still spending the majority of my days down at the farm taking care of my duties there and helping Elaine with whatever chores I could, which included looking after Amanda.

Before the snow flew that autumn, I began assembling material that would be needed — material that would be impossible or difficult to get from the surrounding forest and would have to be brought in from the farm below. In the "impossible" category were roofing tin, two wood-burning stoves, stovepipes, a sink, windows, and nails. In the "difficult" category were mainly things made of wood that would have been just too much trouble to make up on site, such as hemlock planks for the floor, the roof, and the bunks, pine planks for making the door, and spruce planks for the four steps leading onto the front porch. My plan was to haul this material from the farm as far as possible with our small Ford tractor pulling a two-wheeled wagon and leaving the material in the forest over winter for the following year's building season. For the second building season, however, most of the material on the list would not be needed immediately, but I would need at least some planks for a temporary floor to facilitate construction.

"As far as possible" with my small Ford tractor was a little less than a kilometre from the cabin site. All the material was dumped there, and every time I went in to the cabin site, I would carry as much as I could over the trail. That first fall, I made one trip from the farm to the material dump with my tractor to haul in the floor planks I needed for the following year's work and declared the first construction season closed for the winter.

The second year, in April of 1978, building started again after the maple-syrup operation was put to bed. On my first trip to the cabin site, I started carrying in the hemlock floor planks that had been left in the material dump the previous year. There were some fifty-four logs floating all around the lake that had to be corralled. Fortunately, many of them had ended up on the north shore not far from where the cabin was being built. These were left for the moment; they would be easier to retrieve by swimming with them when the water got warmer. In late April it was still too cold to do that. The rest I herded over using a rubber life raft, tying the logs five or six in a string and rowing like mad to tow them to the building site. It took a lot of effort to get them started, but once they got moving it was easy to keep them going.

Eventually, all fifty-four logs were high and dry on shore and enough planks from the material dump had been carried in to lay a sub floor as a working surface inside the four foundation logs. But before laying the planking, the fourteen floor joist logs running from one side of the cabin to the other had to be notched into the two side foundation logs to support the floor planks. The rest of the second year's construction season was taken up by trimming, notching, and raising into place the remaining forty logs retrieved from the lake. When the second year's work was finished, the cabin walls had risen to a height of about five and a half feet. I was beginning to sense a cabin rising in front of me now, instead of just a pile of logs.

Meanwhile, on July 27, 1978, our second daughter, Jessica, was born. Over time, we found the farm environment particularly suited to raising our two daughters. Not only did they have a large pony to ride, they also rode the "daddy" sheep, as they called our ram. Rams can be ornery, but the one we kept for breeding was as gentle as, well a lamb. We had started raising sheep for food and sold our surplus lambs to neighbours.

Amanda became a flower girl at an early age, learning the names of many common wildflowers, which she often picked and left in our rural mailbox just outside the farmhouse as a special gift for the mailman. *Clozer, wetch, goddonwod, stwabewy*, and others. On a warm late summer evening, Mandy and I went tractor-camping to a small, open field on top of a hill in the sugar bush in back of the house. She rode in the small wagon with our camping gear while I pulled with my tractor. We built a campfire and

Daughters on the farm. Amanda with a giant puffball, which we ate later, and Jessica with a black kitten, 1981.

136

cooked a small steak each and boiled some potatoes. That experience was useful for getting Amanda started in appreciating the outdoors. Today, she loves going up to the cabin overnight with her husband, Chris.

Jessica became keen on fishing bass in Lake of the Old Uncles. One day, when she was about six or seven, we were all at the lake together and Jessica decided to catch a bass — to land it herself, unhook it, kill it, gut it, and bring it down to the farmhouse to put in the freezer for a special occasion. She did all that herself without accepting help. The special occasion to eat the bass came unexpectedly some time later. We pushed ourselves away from the table after finishing a generous supper one evening and Jessica announced that she had thawed out the fish and that the special occasion had arrived: she was now going to cook the fish for all of us to eat. We didn't have the heart to disappoint her by suggesting a more appropriate time, preferably not just after dessert, so we screwed up our courage, forced down a few small mouthfuls of fish, and pronounced it absolutely delicious, which pleased Jessica no end.

The third year, 1979, I felled, peeled, and threw into the lake the final thirty-two logs. One day, a friend and I portaged my canoe over the access trail to the lake. We marshalled all the logs from wherever they had ended up in the lake and towed them over in bunches of five or six, landing them at the cabin site. That summer was taken up in raising the final logs and transporting material from the farm to the material dump by tractor, and then onward to the cabin site by muscle power. Raising logs became more and more difficult as the height of the cabin increased. By means of ropes and pulleys I was able to put in place all the wall logs by myself, including the tapering gable-end logs, which were particularly challenging as there was very little to support them until the roof went up. These were all nailed together with foot-long spikes and supported by temporary bracing.

The function of the very last seven logs was to solidify the gable ends and support the roofing planks. They, together with two of the foundation logs that were already in place, were the longest logs of all at twenty-five feet. Their length had to cover not only the cabin itself, but, jutting out forward, the front porch as well. The roof logs were also the highest logs of all to place and secure. Thinking that discretion was the better part of valour, I decided to get some help to raise these last logs. A strong, strapping, sixteen-year-old named Sylvain came on board for three days to help me finish building the frame of the cabin. Roof planking and roofing tin I could handle myself, but raising those last roof logs and spiking them in place was a special challenge.

Sylvain was a bit of a natural philosopher. One day while resting from our labour, we got to talking about time. He told me that when he was young, time seemed to go so much more slowly than it did at his now-advanced age of sixteen, and that time moved very quickly for him now. After pondering this philosophical fact for a moment, he raised his head and, looking at me and my greying beard, candidly declared, "Time must really go fast for you, Mr. Kenney, doesn't it?"

Sylvain was also resourceful. A smoker, one day he forgot to bring matches. Being a non-smoker, I couldn't help him there. He lowered his head in thought, and, after a few seconds, brightened up and asked me if he could borrow my chainsaw.

"Sure," I answered, anxious to see how he was going to light the cigarette with my chainsaw.

At the cabin on Lake of the Old Uncles, winter 1980.

138

Sylvain picked up a small twig from the ground and removed the screw-cap of the saw's gasoline tank. He dipped the twig in the gasoline, screwed the cap back on, quickly removed the wire from the spark plug, and held the twig and the spark-plug wire near the plug but not quite touching. Bracing the saw with his feet, he pulled on the starting cord, which created a spark, which lit the gasoline-soaked twig, which he used to light his cigarette. I was impressed.

At the end of the third day, the last logs were finally in place. I stepped back to look at the cabin and was pleasantly startled. For the first time I could now actually see the completed cabin in my mind's eye. All that was missing from the structure were the roofing planks and roofing tin, but they were not necessary to visualize the completed cabin. All the really hard work was finished. The cabin would soon be habitable. My dream would soon be realized. That night in bed I described to Elaine how far the construction had advanced, and how close we were to the end. The vision I had seen after finishing our work had completely excited me. Sleep was long in coming.

The fourth year, 1980, I planked the roof and covered it with roofing tin, laid down a second layer of floor planks with Styrofoam insulation between the layers, put in two windows and the door, installed a sink, put up two chimneys, and completed the hundred-and-one other tasks that went into the finished cabin. A small woodstove was temporarily installed for heating purposes. Elaine made a whole series of hooks out of appropriately shaped small branches nailed to the walls for hanging clothes, dish cloths, towels, etc. She also sewed up some short curtains to cover the open space under the sink.

It was not possible to bring in the large, heavy cookstove over the steep and crooked footpath. A logging contractor who was working in the area helped me bring the stove in on a small, tracked vehicle to drop it off at a spot near the shore just opposite the cabin. By mid-December the ice was strong enough, and with two friends we pulled that heavy hunk of iron across the lake on a toboggan. The last bit of hard labour was to jockey it up the four steps of the cabin and set it in place.

The log cabin on a wilderness lake that I had dreamed about was built. Thoreau built the cabin on Walden Pond for $28.12½. At twelve hundred dollars, the one on Lake of the Old Uncles cost a bit more, but in comparable dollars, not that much more.

Part Five

LIFE WITH A CABIN

IN 1995, ELEVEN YEARS after leaving the farm and moving to Ottawa, sadly, Elaine and I grew in different directions and we finally decided that it was better for us to go our own separate ways. Despite our separation, there is still a healthy friendship between us.

I bring this matter up to indicate that the few events described below and that involved other relationships occurred after 1995.

The cabin has been a source of great pleasure for me over the years since I completed it in 1980. Not the least of that pleasure comes from the fact that the cabin seems to have struck such a positive chord with so many of the visitors that have used it, both French- and English-speaking. The next chapter introduces this serendipitous phenomenon.

OUR INVISIBLE FRIENDS

THE CABIN IS NOT REACHABLE by road. The closest a car can get to it in summer is about a kilometre; after that, there's the narrow footpath. In winter, after the snow has fallen and the dirt road becomes impassable by car, the walk from down below is about five kilometres, sometimes on snowshoes, sometimes on skis, and sometimes on foot, depending on snow conditions.

There are none of what might be called "modern conveniences" such as electricity, telephones, television sets, radios, or running water. A hand pump draws water from the lake in summer. In winter, snow or ice are melted down for water. Furnishings are sparse: a small table and three chairs plus two rocking chairs, a kitchen counter and sink, two bunks on the lower level plus one above, and a propane lamp. The cabin is about as simple, no more, no less, as the cabins on the shores of lakes around St-Rémi some sixty or more years ago when I was a boy. Thoreau's cabin was perhaps somewhat simpler, but not much.

I know from my rural past that a woods cabin should never be locked. One never knows when someone will need a refuge in an emergency, and besides, a lock is considered an insult and an invitation to break in by certain people. If they use violence to get in, why would it stop once they're inside? No, a lock was bad business, and I didn't use one at the cabin. I worried at first, but I needn't have, as succeeding years showed.

Few people knew the cabin existed, so there were few visitors at first. Then more people discovered it by accident when rambling through the woods or while hunting. Bottles and other trash were being left behind along with a mess of dirty dishes in the sink. I put up a sign in French saying to use the cabin, but to please keep it clean, and signed it "Gerard Kenney." With one exception, never again was garbage left behind and the dishes from then on were always clean and put away.

I left a logbook in the cabin for noting my visits in English: the date, who I came with, the work I did there, and other interesting things, such as "200 Canada geese landed and spent the night," or "saw a coyote on the way in to the cabin." Then one day, someone I didn't know visited the cabin and left me a note in French in the logbook. It said that it was very nice of me to let people use the cabin and asked me to please write in French because the writer had trouble with English.

I replied to the note in French and so began an exchange of correspondence with a growing list of people I had yet to meet, but with whom I obviously shared mutual interests. Some of the notes really flattered and pleased me. One woman wrote that she thought I must have a beautiful soul to build such a nice cabin in such a peaceful setting and to let people use it. She even suggested that I leave a picture of myself in the cabin, which I have never done, fearing that it would certainly destroy her illusions.

One day, I noticed that someone had cut a few small trees near the cabin for firewood. I wrote a note in the logbook saying that I did not think trees that could be seen from the cabin should be cut. I also pointed out that beavers had felled a number of beech trees down by the shore a hundred metres or so to the west of the cabin and that it made nice summer sport to drag them into the lake and swim them over to the rock in front of the cabin. I even did that with a couple of trees one hot summer day and left them on the rock just to show what I meant. The next time I visited the cabin, there was a stack of about eight or nine beaver-cut trees lying on the rock by the shore. I cut them up into more manageable metre-and-a-quarter lengths and carried them to the lean-to shelter attached to the back of the cabin to keep them out of the rain.

When I went back to the cabin a few days later, I got a surprise as I approached. I could see a high stack of split stove wood on the inside of the three railings lining the front porch. All the trees I had cut into metre-and-a-quarter lengths had been further bucked up into forty-centimetre lengths, split, and piled neatly on the porch to season. Inside, further surprises awaited me: a feminine touch had been added. Venetian blinds covered the stark nakedness of the two windows. And then the nicest surprise of all: a small wooden cabinet for dishes, glasses, and cups had been brought in and attached to the wall over the sink. All this, done by people I had never met, to a cabin that didn't even belong to them — a cabin owned by a fellow named Kenney, who wrote his notes in English — and by people with names like Sabourin and Laframboise, who left their notes in French. The separatist movement of Quebec was obviously not operating in this neck of the woods.

After several years, I finally met our invisible friends, who turned out to be four strapping young men and their girlfriends, all from the region, and in their late teens or early twenties. The boys were all interrelated either by bloodlines or marriage lines of their parents. The parents of two of them owned a hundred-acre lot adjacent to the southernmost of our three lots. These boys had been brought up to roam the Black Mountain in back of their homes in search of fish and game for the family tables and had grown to love the outdoor life. I sensed in them the same call of the wild that was so evident in my uncles when I lived in St-Rémi, and which they unknowingly transferred to me. These boys loved to spend occasional days and nights in my cabin when I was not there and I welcomed them to do so. They were of the kind that graciously received, but gave as much or more in return. We got along famously and still do. They eventually built a two-storey cabin of their own on the lot adjacent to ours, far enough away that the intervening hills block any transfer of sound between cabins. We visit each other through the forest from time to time. They are good neighbours. One year, for a case of beer that I had to force upon them, in one day they cut up and split two huge white birches that another good neighbour had felled for me because they were leaning dangerously over the cabin. (I couldn't give that neighbour anything for his work. He wouldn't take anything, either.) The result of all this essentially free work was about a three or four year's supply of firewood for my small cabin.

CHAPTER TWO

THE CANOE

WHILE BUILDING THE CABIN, I portaged my old eighty-pound canoe over the winding and steep trail that leads to Lake of the Old Uncles. I used it to tow logs for the cabin walls from across the lake to where the cabin would be. It was easier and quicker than swimming them across as I had done with the first ones.

I bought the canoe when I was a younger man and I could carry it without too much trouble then. Just a few years ago, the canoe seemed heavier with each passing year. I sold it —with regret, after all the miles that we had done together — and bought one that weighs only fifty pounds. Now, even though I am halfway through my eighth decade of life, I can carry it for a mile or more before putting it down. It gives me a great sense of freedom to be able to go to places where few others go, by portaging along rough trails and paddling up small, beaver-obstructed streams from one lake to another. I still admire the traditional cedar-strip canoe of old, the kind that gives a characteristic hollow *thunk* when struck with a paddle, but they are too heavy for me now, and there comes a time in a man's life when it is a matter of compromising, or not going where one wants to go. I compromised a few years ago and bought the

light Kevlar craft that I can still handle easily. It is of a pale-green colour that blends in well with the wilderness. My lightweight canoe has taken me into waters as varied as those of the wild Labrador interior, and the relative civilization of the Ottawa River.

Someone once wrote, "Store your canoe where you can see it and your paddle where you can touch it." I love my canoe, and even in the middle of winter I go into my garage and rub my fingers along the gentle curve of its side, thinking back to the boiling rapids we have ridden together, and times when it bucked like a wild horse, throwing me more than once into the foam-flecked, dancing waves. My thoughts go forward as well to future adventures not yet lived and a gentle sense of apprehension comes over me — a sense similar, except in degree, to the feeling I get just before sliding down the "V" of an unknown rapid. In my bedroom stand two paddles, both made of rich cherry wood. One has seen a few miles of wilderness waters and the other, the twin brother of the first, is still new and of the smoothness of silk when I pass my hand along its length. I think I will keep it that way.

Cultures of many origins were represented in laying the foundation for North America. The Native cultures made essential contributions: the canoe and the trapping of the furs that supported the first economic system of the north. The French culture was represented by the trading company of Revillon Frères and men such as Pierre-Esprit Radison and Médard Chouart Sieur des Groseillers, as well as the countless indefatigable coureurs de bois and the steel-muscled voyageurs that followed in their wake. From the British Isles came the Scotsmen and the English — governors, factors, and traders of the Hudson's Bay Company and the North West Company as well as explorers *sans pareil* — men such as George Simpson, David Thompson, Alexander Mackenzie, and Simon Fraser, all carried by thin vessels of bark from the St. Lawrence River to the extreme northern and western limits of North America.

Canada is a land of much water. Long ago the inhabitants of the north evolved a craft capable of gliding across its countless lakes and rivers that was perfectly in tune with their nomadic needs and with the materials at hand: the birch-bark canoe. This craft, more than any other, was responsible for uniting the far-flung reaches of the North American continent. The union was forged through the combined efforts of First Nations people and Europeans of many origins using the gift of the interior tribes of Native people: a vessel made from the bark of trees.

Were it not for the birch-bark canoe, the history of North America would be greatly different. This wonderful gift from Native minds and bodies enabled men and women to bridge the thousands of kilometres that lay between the east coast and the waters of the Arctic and Pacific oceans. Thus was laid the foundation upon which the building of the countries of this vast continent began.

Although the material of which the Indian canoe was made has changed in modern times, the basic form of the vessel remains the same to this day. It is truly an enduring symbol of North American history, and particularly of the forging of the links that bind the continent into a land of many and varied cultures. The canoe is no longer a vessel of commercial transportation, but it is one that is held dear for spiritual reasons. In the canoe, many rediscover links with their origins as natural beings in touch with a world of nature — origins that sometimes tend to be obscured in our hectic modern lives. The canoe is capable of transporting us to mystical places of great spiritual value where we may renew the wellsprings of our human and natural existence. This is why the canoe is still important to the lives of many, and why it carries on its usefulness to humankind, no longer as a tool of commerce, but now as a means of achieving renaissance of our spiritual selves.

The canoe is the perfect symbol for maintaining intact the priceless North American continent. It is from the perspective of a canoe slipping quietly along the darkening shores of a wilderness lake, when the hush of evening accompanies the setting of the sun, that the spirit of the north is most easily evoked. As darkness gently settles, one can almost hear a faint voyageur chorus filtering down through the softly soughing evergreens and the rustling leaves of the birches and maples:

> *C'est l'aviron qui nous mène, qui nous mène,*
> *C'est l'aviron qui nous mène en haut.*

CHAPTER THREE
THE WINTER LAKE

THE COLD WINDS OF November usher in the first swirling gusts of snowflakes that start seriously robbing the fall lake of its heat. The change in temperature is a reminder to any remaining waterfowl and to the beavers that a layer of ice will soon separate their respective domains and that they had better take the action required of them at this time of the year. The ducks and geese that have tarried must not further delay their flights to warmer climes and the beavers had better complete any last-minute plans for topping up their larder of tender, juicy branches and saplings. Patches of ice soon start skimming over areas of the lake's surface here and there until an overnight cold snap connects them all together into an icy mantle that will blanket the lake for the next five months. It is time to sharpen the skates.

Sometime around mid December the ice has strengthened enough for skaters to safely practise their sport, and if the snows come late that year, as happens fairly often, it is a fine skating rink indeed that is at their disposal at the Lake of the Old Uncles: a thousand feet long and four hundred feet wide. But the skaters had better hurry, for the ice will only be bare for two weeks or so if they are really lucky, and, more likely than not, nearer to no weeks at all.

The varying period when the ice surface is bare of snow is also prime time for enjoying the frozen lake's many voices, especially when the mercury plummets and night sets in. Later on, when several feet of snow have accumulated on the surface, the lake's voices can still be heard, but low and muffled. For the moment, though, full freedom of lake-speech reigns.

Ice is essentially incompressible, and when great pressures are exerted on it, it must crack. The cracked plates of ice rub against each other like miniature tectonic plates, causing mini-icequakes, complete with rumbling and booming protests from the frozen water at being so roughly treated. The cause of the great pressures that squeeze the ice is the action of the earthly thermostat that lowers the temperature at night and raises it in the daytime, just as furnace thermostats do in many of our homes during winter. Ice may be incompressible under pressure, but its volume does change with temperature, shrinking and expanding in volume as do practically all solids. On cold nights, shrinking tends to cause the blanket of ice to pull away from the shore, allowing the water in the space created to freeze and close the gap. When morning comes, the warming sun causes the icy blanket to expand and push against the now-frozen shore, creating tremendous pressures within the horizontal layer of ice. The result is the booming, grumbling, growling, snapping, chirping, and cracking that accompany the warming day. The reverse process, during the period of cooling that nighttime brings, causes great internal tensions in the covering of ice due to the shrinking of the uneven layer, also accompanied by many different shrieks and groans of protest.

In his book *The Walks of Winter*, respected nature writer Edwin Way Teale described the voice of his pond at Trail Wood:

> As I am standing ... a low-pitched booming sound reverberates through the air. It comes from the direction of the pond. Hollow, rolling, it reaches me like the noise of a muffled concussion. We have heard it several times of late. Now I hear it again. It suggests some submerged timber being thrust violently upward against the underside of the ice.
>
> Last night, the temperature dropped to zero [°F]. Already, on this morning of sunshine, it has risen to twenty-two degrees. I assume this sudden change, accentuating

the tensions inherent in the ice, is responsible for the dull cannonading that I hear.

In Walden, Thoreau commented on the voices of his famous pond in winter:

> The cracking and booming of the ice indicate a change of temperature.... The pond began to boom about an hour after sunrise, when it felt the influence of the sun's rays slanted upon it from over the hills; it stretched itself and yawned like a waking man with a gradually increasing tumult, which was kept up three or four hours. It took a short siesta at noon, and boomed once more toward night, as the sun was withdrawing his influence. In the right stage of the weather a pond fires its evening gun with great regularity. But in the middle of the day, being full of cracks, and the air also being less elastic, it had completely lost its resonance, and probably fishes and muskrats could not have been stunned by a blow on it. The fishermen say that the "thundering of the pond" scares the fishes and prevents their biting. The pond does not thunder every evening, and I cannot tell surely when to expect its thundering; but though I may perceive no difference in the weather, it does. Who would have suspected so large and cold and thick-skinned a thing to be so sensitive? Yet it has its law to which it thunders obedience when it should as surely as the buds expand in the spring. The earth is all alive and covered with papillae. The largest pond is as sensitive to atmospheric changes as the globule of mercury in its tube.

One day, in one of the years that the snow came late, Elaine and I, with our two girls, decided to take advantage of the huge skating rink that we knew the lake would be. The first thing we did after arriving at the cabin was build roaring fires in our two stoves to give us a warm environment to relax in after skating. Then we laced up and off we went, gliding merrily over the icy surface of our private rink. As can be expected, the younger fry lasted longer than their parents, and Elaine and I retired to the warm cabin, leaving them to enjoy themselves. I happened to look out the window at one point and got quite a start. The two girls were on hands and knees, bawling their eyes out and scrabbling as fast as they could to reach shore. We heard shrieks of pure panic and cries of, "The lake is cracking, the ice is breaking up."

I knew immediately what was happening and reassured Elaine that there was no danger, as the ice was over a foot thick. The lake had spoken, but the kids had not learned the language yet. Apparently, a pressure-caused fissure had started out from the other side of the lake and had ZZZIPPED! its way over to our side with almost lightening speed and a great shearing noise, passing right under the two skaters.

On cold winter nights the cabin hosts a wonderful bedtime symphony, provided by the icy giant outside the front door settling down to his grumbling, booming sleep accompanied by the crackling and snapping of the woodstove, whose dancing flames paint the walls and ceiling with nature's brush. It's a wonderful light and sound display to drop off to sleep by.

CHAPTER FOUR

TIME WITHOUT BOUNDARIES

"Here we lose the sense of time. It is like eternity — a veritable little niche of paradise. Thank you for letting us discover it."

(Note left by a visitor, Marguerite Lepage, in the logbook of the cabin on the Lake of the Old Uncles.)

IN *REFLECTIONS FROM THE NORTH COUNTRY,* Sigurd Olson wrote a chapter titled "Timelessness"; Edwin Way Teale wrote a book that he called *Days Without Time.* Both these nature writers were exploring a concept of time that recognizes no boundaries. In reality, time is not partitioned into discrete units — it has no boundaries. It is we humans who create artificial boundaries in time by introducing seconds, minutes, hours, schedules, and deadlines, and by doing so, introduce unhealthy tensions in our lives. It is perhaps a cost of doing business in today's "civilized" world, but it deadens the soul.

A country environment, or better yet, a wilderness environment, is far more conducive to the development of a time-without-boundaries ethos.

155

It is a type of time-space we all knew as children, but that most of us forgot as we grew up and became force-fitted into the modern way of life. Even though we have to live and work in a society where time rules us, instead of the other way around, it is possible to counter the stranglehold that time can exercise on us, and we can do this through meditation. Another approach, which in fact can also enhance our meditation experiences, is to court the wilderness. A few years ago, purely by chance, a friend and I experienced the power of the wilderness to reduce time to its true, undistorted nature.

It was in the late summer of 2000 on a canoe trip into the Labrador wilderness with my work friend, Michèle, that we experienced an unplanned, extended period of time without boundaries. I had planned to do this trip with Philip Schubert, my canoeing partner in Labrador the previous year, but three weeks before we were to leave, Phil strained his back and was put out of commission. I was racking my brains trying to find a replacement partner when Michèle, who worked in the same office I did, came to mind. Michèle is a remarkable person with respect to canoeing. For years, canoeing was a burning passion for her and occupied almost all her leisure time. I was impressed when she told me one day that she had undertaken a seven-day solo canoe trip in the wilderness of northern Quebec some years before, running down the river, rapids and all, and camping at night, completely alone. I asked her if she would replace Phil as my partner for the trip. It didn't take her long to agree.

In the latter part of August of that year, Michèle and I drove the two thousand kilometres from Ottawa to Northwest River, Labrador, our departure point. Before leaving Ottawa we had made arrangements with Louie Montague, whom I had met the year before, and his friend Jock Campbell to motorboat us, our canoe, our food, and our equipment up Grand Lake from Northwest River to Louie's tilt on the Nascaupi River, the small cabin I described earlier, which sits at the confluence of the Nascaupi and Red Wine rivers. We intended to paddle some fifteen miles up the Red Wine and then attempt to bushwhack twelve miles or so to the place in the wilderness where Leonidas Hubbard of the Hubbard and Wallace expedition died of starvation in 1903. After that, we would make our way back to Louie's tilt.

Louie dropped us off at his tilt and we arranged with him to return with Jock in ten days to boat us back to Northwest River. It struck us immediately how wild a place we had come to. Fresh tracks in the mud of the beach overlooked by the tilt revealed the recent passage of bear, moose, caribou, wolf, fox, Canada geese, and other, smaller denizens of the Labrador wild.

We had ten days to paddle up the valley of the Red Wine, reach our objective, and get back to the tilt in time for the return trip to Northwest River. The following morning, Michèle and I started up the Red Wine, paddling and lining our canoe for the next day and a half through unusually shallow water, only to find the river level so low that year that it was impractical and even dangerous to go as far upriver as we had planned. We realized with regret that we would have to abort our expedition. That afternoon we turned back downriver and camped on the same wide, sandy beach as on the first night coming up. Early the following afternoon saw us back at our starting point at Louie's tilt. We had been gone three days and we now had a seven-day wait before Louie and Jock came back for us. There was nothing we could do about our situation since we had no means of communicating with our two friends to ask them to pick us up earlier than planned.

Every day, Michèle and I woke up to the invigorating, cold morning air of Labrador in August with morning temperatures hovering around the three-degree-Celsius mark, and afternoons warming up to a level of sixteen to twenty degrees Celsius. During our whole stay, the sky was generally clear with some intermittent clouds and a couple of brief summer showers. We soon became aware that we had attracted the attention of a bird of many names to our outdoor breakfast table: Canada jay, grey jay, whiskey jack, camp robber — take your pick. In fact, there were two or three of them always flitting about. They were very wary at first, but after a while they got up their courage and became quite bold, even flying through the open door of the tilt to peck at our bread supply inside. They are not called "camp robbers" for nothing.

We also attracted the attention of a number of scurrying red squirrels looking for a handout. When we prepared our rolled oats for breakfast, we began cooking up twice as much as we needed for ourselves; the rest was for the wildlife. We had enough to easily last us seven days, even at double rations every morning. For an hour or more every day over breakfast, we were entertained by a wonderful circus of whiskey jacks and squirrels squabbling over the oatmeal we put out for them. We eventually had the birds for fairly close company as they gently floated down on silent wings to land softly beside us on our picnic table. They pecked at the oatmeal pot on the table while the squirrels ran around nervously on the ground where we had placed another pot for them. Birds and squirrels sometimes met at the same pot in innocent confrontation as neither was really a menace to the other.

Every day, breakfast became a special event for us. We lingered for a long time in the company of our morning visitors just for the pleasure of it. Cleaning up the dishes afterwards was also part of the events of the morning. We went down to the river and washed them on the sandy beach. I would go for a short swim while we were down there. The river was slightly muddy — a bit too muddy for Michèle — but we solved that problem. Down river a few hundred feet, a clear, bubbling stream rushed down from the mountains to end up in the broad Nascaupi. The stream had a couple of small, deep pools in it, each about as big as a bathtub, where we could immerse ourselves for our afternoon ablutions. We waited until the warmer air temperature of the afternoons before braving the bracing mountain waters. It took a bit of time to get in, but once in, it was thoroughly enjoyable as well as invigorating. However, though our tensions and worries were at a low, we found out that it did not mean we could afford to become careless.

One day I encountered an exciting, though frightening, phenomenon on the shore of the Nascaupi that I knew of, as everyone does, but had never actually experienced or even seen before: a quicksand bog. It looked like a continuation of the hard sand that I was walking on along the river's edge, but when I stepped on it, there was no support at all, and my right leg went in above the knee. Luck was with me in that it was not an extensive bog, and my left leg and hands remained on solid ground as I fell. The suction on the right leg was strong, but, with considerable effort and using the purchase of the hard sand within reach, I was able to pull myself out. From then on I was very, very careful about where I stepped.

Finding things to do was not a problem. One afternoon we canoed higher up the Nascaupi River to the foot of some rapids that would have made it difficult to continue. We tried fishing the rapids, but without success. Then we explored a good-sized island downstream of the tilt that appeared to be a haven for bears, judging from the numerous tracks in the soft sand, although we did not see any bears. As mentioned, the beach where the tilt was located bore not only bear tracks, but also those of wolves, moose, caribou, fox, and Canada geese, though we never actually saw any of these animals except geese. Another day, we hiked several miles along an old, mossy Indian trail that originates behind Louie's tilt and which had been his trapline until he gave it up a few years ago.

What Michèle and I didn't realize at first was that we had fallen into an extended and unplanned period of time without boundaries. There were no deadlines, no schedules. Our time-space was not divided into days; it flowed continuously, slipping into and out of periods of more or less activity according to whether it was light or dark. In his chapter on *Timelessness* from *Reflections from the North Country* Olson wrote, "When one finally arrives at the point where schedules are forgotten, and becomes immersed in ancient rhythms, one begins to live.

In Olson's terms, we had arrived and were truly living.

&

Across the Nascaupi from Louie's tilt is a log cabin his brother built several years ago. It is where his brother died suddenly one day just a few years before while enjoying the wilderness. A bronze plaque is nailed on the outside of the cabin in his honour. The rocky shore in front of the cabin was littered with fascinating geological formations called "concretions," of which we brought back a number of samples to show my geologist friend Ilde in Ottawa. Ilde explained that concretions are formed by calcite or silica-rich groundwater that deposits these minerals on particles of a different material, and these particles act as nuclei around which the concretions form.

Those days waiting for our ride back to Northwest River were seven of the most serene and restful days of my adult life. Not since I was a child had my mind been so carefree and curious about my surroundings. There was nothing we could do about our situation. There was nothing to worry about, there were no computers, no telephones, no televisions, no radios, no newspapers, none of that gamut of things that we can't seem to do without in the city. We had no commitments, no responsibilities to fulfill, and we were not rushing to go anywhere. And yet, there was not a moment of boredom in any of those days.

On the morning of the seventh day, our period of time without boundaries was drawing to a close and we knew that we would soon have to re-enter the world of seconds, minutes, hours, schedules, and deadlines. Neither of us felt quite ready to go back to that world and our hearts grew heavy at the sight of our boatmen in the distance, chugging up the river, coming to take us back to civilization.

Our reintegration was quick and brutal. We soon learned that during our interlude of personal serenity, a terrible event had taken place in the world that had horrified everyone for days on end and its effect was still being felt. The Russian submarine *Kursk* had sunk to the bottom of the sea with every member of its crew. Over a period of several days, attempts to rescue the crew had been unsuccessful. There were no survivors. It was indeed a terrible accident. For a week or more, the attention of the whole world was riveted on the horrible fate of those poor Russian sailors. It occurred to me that while this tragedy played out, Michèle and I had been blissfully unaware of it, and even had we been aware, we could not have changed anything.

As a professional in the field of communications, I have often wondered to what extent the communications revolution has improved our lives and to what extent it has robbed us of our peace of mind. Has the degree of connectedness introduced into our lives by modern inventions such as television, cell phones, the internet, call waiting, telephone answering machines, and others made us utterly dependent on being in instant communication with almost everyone and anyone in the so-called civilized world? Has it so robbed us of our independence that being incommunicado for a time becomes almost a panic situation? Are we perhaps so overloading our brains with clutter that the important things do not receive the attention they should? Do we really need to know instantaneously and in great detail through the news media all the horrible occurrences that take place in every dark corner of the world every day? How can we expect to have serene days, joyous days, when every day we not only wake up to reports of the horrors of our world in the newspapers and radio or TV programs, but in the case of many of us, we close our days with a repetition of those same horrors plus new ones on the eleven o'clock news? What did Michèle and I lose by not knowing, until a week or so after the fact, that the *Kursk* had sunk while we were living our serene days of time without boundaries? Nothing. There was nothing we could have done about it in any case. Even in 1845, Thoreau in *Walden* complained about the instant news syndrome when he observed that, "Hardly a man takes a half-hour's nap after dinner, but when he wakes he holds up his head and asks, 'What's the news'?"

In *Walden*, Thoreau foresaw the frivolous use that our communications inventions would be put to when he wrote,

> We are eager to tunnel under the Atlantic and bring the old world some weeks closer to the new; but perchance the first news that will leak through into the broad, flapping American ear will be that the Princess Adelaide has the whooping cough.... Our inventions are wont to be pretty toys which distract our attention from serious things. They are improved means to an unimproved end.

We can hardly be said to be living in a time-space without boundaries when our minds are continually bombarded by bits of unconnected information from here, there, and everywhere, all vying for our immediate attention in bits of disjointed time, each with its limiting borders.

I am by no means an expert on transcendental meditation, nor am I an accomplished practitioner of the art. However, from personal experience with the modest periods of time I spend in meditation, I believe that this technique holds great promise for quieting the mind and preventing negative energy from the past, and about the future, from intruding in our thought processes when we are trying to live in the now. I believe that the quiet mind achieved through meditation goes hand-in-hand with building a healthy living space of time without boundaries.

Michèle, with Louie on her left and Jacques on her right, boating down the Nascaupi River as we left Louie's cabin to return to Northwest River and civilization.

CHAPTER FIVE

THE SERENE WOODS

ECKHART TOLLE IS A MAN of German origin who, according to his writings, led a life of desperation and anxiety in his younger days — a life that took him dangerously close to suicide at one stage. At the age of twenty-nine, for reasons he himself did not understand, Tolle went through a profound spiritual transformation that left him in a state of deep peace, joy, and enlightenment. Tolle had been living in Vancouver, B.C., since 1996, when he wrote a book entitled *The Power of Now*.

Put simply, Tolle's thesis is that there is a past, a present, and a future for all of us. The present is what he calls the "Now," an infinitesimally short period of time, which nevertheless is the only time space in which we truly live. He points out that we do not live in the past, nor do we live in the future. We can only live in the Now. Logically, the Now should be of supreme importance to us. Yet, many, if not the majority, of thoughts that occupy our minds on a daily basis are either from the past, or they are projections about the future. Many of these thoughts are either negative preoccupations about what is past, or projections of unsatisfied desires and fears about the future. They are not part of our Now and they are destructive to our enjoyment of the Now. Tolle teaches that the full power and enjoyment of our Now can only be achieved by quieting the mind and eliminating those troublesome thoughts from the past and future — in other words, to really live in the Now with as little interference as possible from the past and future in our thoughts.

This is not a new idea. Thoreau expressed much the same concept in different words when he wrote:

> Both for bodily and mental health, court the present —
> Time hides no treasures; we want not its then but its now
> — Above all, we cannot afford not to live in the present.
> He is blessed over all mortals who loses no moment of
> the passing life in remembering the past.

Anne Morrow Lindbergh once spent an extended period of solitary introspection in a cabin by the sea. During this period she wrote a slim and delightful volume, *Gift From the Sea*, in which she experienced, as she described it, "the joy in the now ... the peace in the here."

The concept of living in the here and now is the very principle on which Buddhist meditation is founded. One of the basic goals of Buddhist meditation is the quieting of the mind by concentrating it on something in the present to the exclusion (as much as is humanly possible) of negative, intruding thoughts about the past and the future. What Tolle describes in *The Power of Now* resembles very closely certain aspects of Buddhist thinking on meditation.

Distractions from the past and future are not the only intrusions that can disturb one's efforts at meditation, though. There are distractions of the here and now as well. Some Buddhists who have reached very advanced levels of meditation practice can meditate successfully, it has been said, under almost any circumstances, even those including blaring sirens, loud music, jackhammers in the street, or worse. However, I am sure that the vast majority would find it difficult to meditate under such circumstances. In fact, the quieter the better is certainly the way most of us feel about our surroundings when meditating. There appears to be a common bond linking serenity, solitude, and silence. Serenity, or quieting of the mind, is more easily achieved in conditions of silence and solitude by most people.

Silence is an environmental state. Natural silence includes the sounds of nature, but not of man. When Sigurd Olson wrote a chapter titled "The

Great Silences" in *Reflections from the North Country,* he was referring to the silences that existed before the advent of man and precluded the noises of the modern world, but included "the rushing of water, the crash of waves against the shore, the roar of avalanches on mountain slopes, of wind through the trees, the howling of wolves, the bugling of elk when the aspen are gold in the foothills, the myriad sounds of birds and insects." It is this kind of silence that I value for meaningful meditation, a silence that is devoid of the noises of man, but replete with the sounds of nature. Noises that intrude on one's mental or physical context when meditating, or writing, are a bothersome distraction. The sounds at the cabin are, with few exceptions, natural sounds, and far from being distractions, they promote quieting of the mind. The silence that reigns at the Lake of the Old Uncles is the kind that includes the lapping of waves against the rocks, the soughing of wind in the branches of trees, the slapping of beaver tails on the surface of the lake, the croaking of frogs, the singing and twittering of birds as they flit through the trees.

Solitude is a physical state, the state of being alone, and can occur in a variety of places, even cities. I believe there is also a special type of solitude, which I call *solitude à deux,* when two like-minded people can share a state of physical solitude without diminishing that state for the other.

Fall at Lake of the Old Uncles, 1992.

The crashing of thunder and great bolts of lightning accompanied by the acrid smell of ozone are weather extremes that are part — an exciting part — of the wilderness experience. John Muir would climb to the top of the tallest pine trees when a good blow was in the offing, the better to appreciate the powerful force of the gusty wind blowing him smartly back and forth as his tree top was powerfully bent in one direction, only to spring back in the other with each gust. Surely, one cannot speak of serenity under such conditions. That is so, but being part of violent nature does not contradict the concept of serenity. John Muir surely felt serene *after* climbing down from a tall pine following a storm, having lived through a spiritual experience — similar, perhaps, to what one feels shortly after successfully running a wild and powerful, white-water rapid in a canoe. Serenity and excitement don't necessarily go together at the same moment in time, but one can enhance the other.

A remarkable feature of serenity is the complete lack of physical tension in the body. Because of the lack of tension, bodily movement is at a minimum. One fits into the natural world in a seamless way and animal life reacts as if one weren't there. One seems to blend in smoothly with nature, without any rough edges. The serenity of being in quiet nature greatly enhances what can be observed of the natural world. There are thousands of things going on around us when in a natural environment, but many of these things go unnoticed or are interrupted by our mere presence, especially when we are not in a quiet and serene mood. Of course, we cannot always be in such a mood. There are things to be done, wood to be chopped, repairs to be made, meals to be cooked, songs to be sung. But time set aside to be quiet and not busying about can be very rewarding. It is then, as if by magic, that the truly fascinating side of the wilderness fearlessly emerges as nature assumes its normal rhythms.

In the very early spring, when the woods and ponds are just coming back to life after yet another winter's sleep, especially as the cool of evening comes on, the air begins to vibrate with mating songs so loud, shrill, and strident that one may be excused for thinking the originators of the songs must be of quite impressive size. As one nears the source, the sheer volume of the cacophony is deafening to the point that it overloads the human hearing system. On approaching the source more closely, strangely, the sound dies down and stops, while the songs from sources farther away can still be heard at a more comfortable level. All that is seen is a marshy pond, just like so many others, yet this one is silent now. The originators of the songs are nowhere to be seen nor heard. But if one hunkers down and has the patience to wait, in a little while, tentative peeps begin to be heard again from the silenced pond. If one waits quietly and motionless long enough, the frogs, for that is what they are, become reassured that what they had perceived as danger a few moments ago, has passed. Soon they are peeping again for all they are worth, to the distress of one's ears. These singers are a species of tree frog known as *Hyla crucifer*, or spring peeper — *crucifer* because of a dark "X's" on their backs. Far from being big, they are only about three and a half centimetres long and it is a marvel that such a loud song can come from such small creatures.

Peepers are not easy to see. My young daughter Amanda approached me at the cabin one day many years ago, hands cupped one over the other, obviously holding something she wanted to show me. As she separated her hands slowly, I saw a black "X" on the back of a small frog. It was the first peeper I had ever seen, and I have seen very few since. A child often disturbs nature much less than an adult.

⤢

Earlier I wrote of *solitude à deux*. On a calm and warm, sunny summer afternoon, a friend and I shared a period of such solitude at the cabin while sitting on a rock at the very edge of the lake, our feet almost touching the water. For more or less an hour, we sat there without moving, without uttering a word, lost in our own thoughts, oblivious of the presence of the other as we absorbed the serenity of the moment. We must have blended in well with the natural scene, enough that a bullfrog at the water's edge, just inches from our feet, went about its normal business as if we were not there, and provided us with a view of that business, which neither of us had ever witnessed before — nor since, in my case.

The bullfrog came slowly out of the bush and stepped onto the very rock we were sitting on, just a foot or so away from our feet, not hopping as frogs usually do, but stealthily crawling step by careful step, as a cat does when stalking a mouse. Like a cat, the frog was hunting its prey. The air was filled with flying insects, the most prominent of which were large, steel-grey-and-black dragonflies flitting about our heads, diaphanous wings reflecting nuggets of golden sun.

The frog was quite aware of a dragonfly habit of landing on the rocks to rest. At one point, as the frog neared the water's edge, it stopped its stalking crawl and settled into a waiting period, carefully positioning its hind feet underneath its body by slowly stamping them up and down, again, much like a cat does before its final and deadly spring onto its prey. One of the flitting dragonflies made the fatal mistake of landing on our rock not far from the frog. In a flash, the frog's powerful hind legs sprang like a catapult cut loose and propelled their owner, mouth agape, toward the hapless dragonfly. Together, hunter and prey tumbled head over heels into the lake. When the frog emerged from the water and crawled, dripping wet, back onto the rock, there were a couple of centimetres of the dragonfly's black tail sticking out the side of its mouth. The amphibian crawled back into the bushes to finish its lunch. My friend and I looked at each other with amazement and joy that we had been able to share this little bit of tragic, natural drama, right at our toe tips. Had we not been serenely quiet, we would never have been allowed to see this marvellous scene.

I once came upon a pair of garter snakes one warm spring day with their bodies lying against each other in a straight line on the ground, not in sinuous curves as they are normally seen. They were obviously in a mating embrace. Only their heads were raised above the ground, swaying back and forth in an ecstatic dance. I slowly approached and crouched within a foot or two of them without eliciting the least sign that they were aware of my presence. The mating continued for several minutes, but when it was over, their rush to slither away made it obvious that they were now quite aware of me. However, the threat of my presence so close to them must have been a weaker force than was the joy of their mating. It seemed to have been a question of first-things-first, and preservation of the species had prevailed over individual flight. Mating of wild animals is not often seen, probably because the act puts them in a vulnerable position with respect to predators, with humans normally being looked upon as potential predators; but a quiet and unobtrusive human being will be tolerated if one remains still.

One spring day at the lake, I witnessed two unusual froggy dramas within minutes of each other. As I sat quietly on the porch of the cabin, I became aware of a disturbance a few metres away along the trail to the cabin by the water's edge. The situation looked very strange from where I sat. There appeared to be a large bull frog jumping with great kicks of its hind legs, it seemed, but jumping in a very unusual way. It was jumping crazily, straight up in the air at times, landing every which way, sometimes upside-down, sometimes on its side. Sometimes it even seemed to do a complete somersault. "What is going on here?" I wondered to myself. "Is this frog having a seizure?" I got up quietly, slowly slipped down the four cabin steps to the ground, and carefully approached the scene of the commotion. As I got closer, the cause of the mysterious gymnastics became clear. The bullfrog was indeed being propelled erratically in all directions by a pair of hind legs, but not its own. Sticking out of its mouth were the legs of a smaller frog in the process of being swallowed, with which it did not agree at all. It was doing all the jumping in a last ditch effort to avoid its fate — unsuccessfully, I have to say. I had read that bullfrogs were cannibals; here was proof positive. It was a bit of a hard lesson for the smaller frog, but a wonderful nature lesson for me.

Shortly after, I noticed another commotion along the trail, this time in the water. I could see a round area of the water's surface, about twenty centimetres in diameter, that seemed to be boiling. Another mystery to be solved, I thought as I approached slowly. Ten smaller frogs, perhaps green frogs (of which there are many in the lake), were stretched out flat on the surface of the water, all in a circle, heads inward toward the centre, desperately kicking the water up into a froth with their hind legs like so many little outboard motors. All but one, that is. The one that wasn't kicking was in the middle of the circle, not moving, but being continuously butted by the heads of the nine kickers. "What in heaven's name is going on here?" I asked myself. Sitting there watching this spectacle, I finally came to the conclusion that, this being mating season, I was probably witnessing the thrashings of nine male frogs trying to mate with one poor female in the middle. A gang-bang, as it might be called. I felt sorry for the quiet one, but she may have been quite happy about the situation for all I know. I must verify this tentative conclusion with a biologist some day.

My conclusion about the froggy gang-bang was strengthened when I was fortunate enough one spring day to see an almost identical performance, but by a completely different species of animal: mallard ducks. The bangers were quite obviously male mallards with their bottle-green heads, while the bangee was a single brown-feathered female. I thought that she must certainly be killed since she seemed to be almost continuously under water as her lovers mated with her one after the other by grabbing her by the nape of the neck with their bills and violently thrusting the poor bird underwater to mount her; all the while everyone in the gang was fighting desperately to be next to have a go at her. Things did eventually calm down, though, and out swam Ms. Mallard from the scene of violence, apparently no worse for the wear as she smoothed down her feathers, straightening out her clothes and picking the hay out of her hair, so to speak, while the males raced about at top speed hither and thither in great excitement.

Twice in late September, I have spotted a mallard couple performing what looked like a mating ritual. Strange time of the year for mating, I thought. The ritual began with much raising and lowering of heads and necks, sometimes in step, sometimes not, as the two swam close to each other. Both times the males were splendid in their newly acquired winter plumage. After a minute or so of this preliminary, in both cases, the males sidled up to the females, grabbed them from behind by the neck with their bills and climbed onto their backs, completely submerging them. Several seconds of excited movement ensued, after which the females each emerged and went about their business straightening out their feathers while the males raced around the surface of the water in all directions. The experience seemed to have dramatically charged the males with energy. The only explanation I could come up with was that they had mated, but in September? Why not; man is not the only animal to mate in all seasons.

Bigger game than mallards and frogs have found the quietude of the lake and cabin to be non-threatening, even when someone is there, so long as there is no movement or noise. In the far south-western corner of the lake, a game trail comes up from the valley below. Deer and moose are often seen there. The moose especially, sometimes walk into the lake and swim across to some other point along the shore to get out there and continue their ramblings along other forest game trails. There is such a trail that starts at the water's edge some seven metres in front of the cabin, where moose come out of the lake, and meander past the cabin porch within touching distance, if anyone is on the porch.

One quiet spring afternoon I was sitting on the porch reading when a movement caught my eye. I saw what, at that distance and to the naked eye, looked like a large, brown bird waving its uplifted wings in all directions, most un-bird like. I carefully lifted my binoculars to my eyes. Some bird. It was a pair of moose's ears, and the almost-completely submerged animal was swimming straight for the cabin. I took the greatest care to be quiet and immobile. Steadily, on came the moose and I was certain it was heading for the game trail that begins just a few metres from where I sat. As the beast approached I could see from the velvety knobs on its head that it was a male, but of what size I had no idea as its body was completely underwater. On it came, and though I didn't move and made no noise, there was one thing I couldn't control: my scent. I suspect the animal got a whiff of me. It came right to the rock and was about to step out onto it when it sniffed the air, turned, and swam back to the far side of the lake. With my binoculars, I watched it rise out of the water on the far shore — some two hundred metres away at that point — and I saw that it was a huge bull. It would have been truly impressive had it emerged from the water at my feet.

A few weeks later, a mature moose got even closer to my friend André, who also was alone at the cabin at the time. While sitting on the porch in a rocking chair, he watched a moose calmly round the corner of the cabin between a bush and the porch railing just a few feet away from him, go down to the shore of the lake, sniff a few times, then cross from left to right across the front of the cabin and silently melt into the wilderness. André's heart was impressed. It took a few moments to resume its normal idling speed. The following day, the moose came back in the opposite direction, and for its own reasons, passed in back of the cabin this time, instead of in front.

These woodsy dramas all took place within fifty-five miles, an hour and a bit, from downtown Ottawa, as my friends and I spent quiet moments enjoying the solitude and serenity of the cabin and its environs.

CHAPTER SIX

THE LOGBOOK SPEAKS

IN 1981, ONE YEAR AFTER the cabin was finished, I left a logbook on a shelf in the new dwelling and in this logbook I made notes of my visits: what I did, who I came with, what I saw or heard of note, and any other interesting titbits. Then one day, some passing woods wanderers, whom I did not know, left me a note in the logbook that started a fascinating and ongoing interchange between me and a good many other passersby in my absence. Some of these people I got to know over the years, but there are a number I still have not met to this day.

A sampling taken from those notes on the wildlife I saw at the lake that first year shows the remarkable diversity and number of wild animals in that area in those early days. Human activity on the Black Mountain has not changed to any appreciable degree since then. There was very little of it then and there is very little of it now, yet over the years since 1981 the amount of wildlife that can be seen on an average day at the lake has dropped drastically, as the logbook entries show. I wish to start this chapter by quoting entries made during that first year, 1981. The very first entry in the book was by me on May 3rd:

May 3

As I arrived at the beaver pond across the Black Mountain road, a lone Canada goose began slowly swimming away nonchalantly, and after ten or fifteen seconds, she took off with a single honk, headed in the direction of the lake. As I arrived at the lake, two ducks whirred away and two Canadas lifted off, honking as they flew to the west end of the lake. Then a whole flock started honking as they took off from the west end of the lake and just as soon set down again right in front of me at the east end of the lake. They swam back to the west end of the lake. I continued on to the cabin and flushed a pair of wood ducks and heard a beaver slap its tail.

7 PM DST. Counted forty-two geese. Other flocks flew overhead, but the geese on the lake paid them no mind. Then three more came in for a landing. After a short exchange of news, all quieted down again. A lone duck came out of nowhere and landed at the west end of the lake. As I was having supper, the flock started honking and took off to the east. But three of their members stayed behind. Were these the last three that had come in? A croaking great blue heron flapped slowly overhead. I kept hearing honking from the direction of the beaver pond to the east.

No Canada geese have landed on the lake for six years now during our May visits. In 2007, none even overflew the lake.

May 13–14

Overnighting with Don Norris. Early evening three moose (a cow and two yearlings) put in at the west end of the lake and swam to a point opposite the cabin, a bit to the east.

June 9–10

On the evening of the 9th I scared a beaver up on land just after crossing his dam. [In a panic, he dove into the lake.] Did he ever make tracks for the water. I could follow his underwater progress by the bubbles he kept sending up. On the morning of the 10th I was visited by a curious otter. He kept circling around for quite a while, all the time giving short, explosive bursts of air followed by a kind of moan.

June 17-18

Saw a muskrat and a beaver. The muskrat presents more of his back above water than either the beaver or the otter. You can see the rat's tail as it swims. In the morning a racoon was down by the rock in front of the cabin.

June 23

Saw a spider lurching along rather unsteadily. Upon closer examination, it appeared to be carrying a black ant. The spider was ten if not twenty times larger than the ant. As I approached, the ant scurried away. "Aha!" I thought. "I scared the spider and the ant escaped." Looking at it more closely, I found the spider to be quite dead. In fact, it was the ant that had been carrying the spider.

June 28

Went to fish the trout lake with Richard Despatie and flushed a deer fawn going down the hill at the west end of our lake. When we came back about three hours later we flushed it again in the same spot.

June 29

A bear cub went bounding across the road as I was driving home in the evening.

June 30

Caught two good-sized bass casting just in front of the cabin.

July 25

Saw a bullfrog gobble up a smaller frog with a tremendous struggle.

The number of birds we saw and heard in those early days was marvellous. The spring warblers were a joy to observe — redstarts, Blackburnians, ovenbirds, water thrushes, black-throated blues, myrtles, chestnut-sideds, and others. In the fields were meadowlarks, bobolinks, stooping snipes, and many other species. At night we heard and called barred owls, which answered our calls. In 2007, few if any of these birds can be seen or heard. Alas, Rachel Carson's "Silent Spring" appears to be very close to an accomplished reality on the Black Mountain. Our spring notes on wildlife at the cabin are sparse indeed in 2007 compared to the early 1980s.

Summer at the Lake of the Old Uncles cabin, 1994.

On the other hand, the logbook records interesting developments on the human side of things. For the first seven years, I was the only person who made entries in the logbook. But then, on May 21, 1988, the following note in perfect English appeared in the book:

> We came here and our names are Stephane, Martin, and Eric. We first saw this cabin last winter so we decided to come fishing. We saw a big trout but we didn't catch it. We thank you for lending us your cabin [unknowingly

on my part — author] for one night. Very nice weather but too many flies. We caught a catfish in the morning, we saw lots of duck. Thank you.

(unsigned)

I make a point of remarking on the perfect English because the Black Mountain is in an area of Quebec that is 99.9 per cent French-speaking and the names of the visitors are without doubt of three Francophones.

Then, a few months later, on September 4 of the same year, another note appeared in the logbook from two more perfectly bilingual Francophones:

We came up here to relax and get away from the civilization. We arrived at 4:30 p.m.; it was raining and a sleepy day. Going to a party tonight so have to sleep and came here. By the way, who owns this place?

First time here but not the last. Hope you don't mind us coming here. It's a very beautiful place. Whoever built this place did a great job.
Signed: Steph Chartrand and Hugues Rochon

These notes were the first of many such notes left in the logbook along with mine over the following two decades — notes written by people I did not know when they first signed in. I did finally meet a handful or two of these people, and with a small number I have become good friends.

On October 8, 1990 a note of some significance appeared in the logbook. It was written in French by a young lady who had been to school with my daughter, Amanda, when we lived on the farm some years earlier. I did not know her, but she knew who I was. She ended her note in French with the following words, which I have translated:

If you remember who I am, please answer me, but if you can write in French, it would help me a lot. Thank you!
Signed: Pascale S.

Writing in French is not a problem for me, so I did answer her as she wished and from then on, I wrote my entries sometimes in French and sometimes in English. The significance of Pascale's note was that, now, even those Francophones who could not manage English too well, but were interested in what I was doing on the Black Mountain, could contribute freely in French and they did. It was as if a floodgate had been opened.

It was on a day in November 1995 that the miraculous pile of cut-up firewood appeared on the cabin porch. Inside was a small, wooden dish-and-utensil cabinet nailed to the wall over the sink and venetian blinds over the windows. I rushed over to the logbook on the kitchen table and flipped the pages to find out who my benefactors were. A very modest note from three gentlemen and a lady I had never met, but whom I knew of from their previous notes, informed me (in French) that,

> We have given you some blinds so you can sleep longer in the morning. We will surely come back to cut up the rest of the beaver-felled trees. Thank you once again, Mr. Kenney.
> Signed: Sébastien, Nancy, Jean-François, and Étienne

Them thanking *me*! And they didn't even mention the dish and cutlery cabinet they had installed! And the wood they had cut! They were thanking *me* for letting them use the cabin. I had to find out who these people were. But before I could, the three gentlemen struck again on December 9th and 10th of the same year, writing in French:

> We came to overnight at the cabin to relax as well as to clean up and replace the stove pipe, which has become hazardous. We were happy to find out [from a note I had left them] that you appreciated the improvements we made to the cabin. That quite pleased us.
> Signed: Étienne, Sébastien, and Jean-François

It was not before the following June that I finally met them and found out who these three Musketeers were. I was at the cabin with my friend Doug from Quebec City on our annual three-day spring retreat in the wilderness when they showed up. I found them surprisingly young to have such a well-developed sense of responsibility and love of nature — either late teens or early twenties. Their parents, whom I found out I knew from our ten years on the farm, had obviously brought them up in a healthy environment of country authority and love of nature. Eventually, the three boys built their own cabin over the hills on a lot adjacent to ours, out of sight and earshot. We visit each other through the woods at times. They no longer use our cabin, but since I don't live close by anymore, they occasionally visit it when there is no one there just to keep tabs on it for me and make sure everything is in order. Real gentlemen!

Many entries commented on how the writers found they could achieve peace and serenity, and how they could relax and recharge their batteries in the isolation and quietude of the cabin and the lake, and they thanked me profusely for enabling them to enjoy those pleasures. I got much satisfaction from reading those words, because I knew exactly how they felt and I was pleased that I could offer them the same pleasures that I derived from the cabin.

I would like to end this chapter on two wonderful notes: a message that pleased me, which I have translated, and a sketch of my cabin, both left in the logbook by a lady I have not yet had the pleasure of meeting, Jézabel St-Louis:

Sunday, February, 2000

1st time I come to the cabin and I am staying for a week; this place is really more than I expected. I believe I shall live a weeklong dream here. I really pushed myself to get to the cabin through three feet of snow, but I feel that I will not regret it. Thank you truly, Mr. Kenney, you are a really an exceptional person (even if I have never met you).

Jézabel

Sketch of the Cabin on Lake of the Old Uncles atop a fantasmagorical world, left in the logbook by visitor Jezabel St-Louis, in 2000.

Part Six

SHIFTING GEARS

ALTHOUGH THE COUNTRY was good for the children when they were young, Elaine and I foresaw that there would be important disadvantages to staying in that environment as they grew older. There are certain aspects of the city that are essential for young people to grow. Access to adequate education is one of them, exposure to cultural aspects of life is another. There was another issue that concerned us, and that was our inability to make adequate money as subsistence farmers to properly take care of the needs of our two growing daughters. We decided that it was time to leave the country and return to the city.

In 1982, I took steps to increase the earning power of our family in preparation for moving to Ottawa. Over the next year, I launched and operated a small technical translation business which I called DocuTech. Translation was a field I had a bit of experience in, but now I got serious about it. An acquaintance in Ottawa was the owner and CEO of an engineering company that needed someone to translate operating manuals for telecommunications equipment from English to French. I signed a contract with him for the task, which I could do at home on the farm. I knew this contract would not last forever, so I kept my ears open for other translation possibilities with an eye to the future. By chance one day, I met on an Ottawa street a long-time friend I had not seen for years who told me about a possible opportunity at the Ministry of Veterans Affairs. The work consisted of translating the operating and maintenance manuals for their computer systems from English to French. It was a fair-sized job and I was told that, to meet the requirements of the contract, I would have to provide two other translators in addition to myself. I told them that I could do that. What my prospective employers did not know was that, right in front of their eyes, I had just jumped off another of Ray Bradbury's cliffs and I would now be building my wings on the way down. I did not know any other available translators, let alone technical translators.

I contacted the Translation Department at the University of Ottawa and asked if they knew of any just-graduated translators looking for jobs. The university told me of two young women in that category whom they could recommend, except that they had no particular skills in computer systems. I was not surprised, nor worried, by that — I was prepared for it. My plan was that the women would provide their freshly minted language skills and I would provide my technical knowledge as well as my translation experience. We would also edit each other's work, which is an important factor for ensuring quality of translation.

I had the two young ladies submit to short tests to verify their translation skills — tests they passed with flying colours. I was awarded the overall contract, signed subcontracts with my two translators, and we were in business. The reaction of one of them when I told her how much I would be paying her was, "*Mais c'est énorme!*" — "But that's enormous!" We were provided an office in the Ministry of Veterans Affairs building in downtown Ottawa and started on our project. As the family name of one was Marin and of the other, Dulac, I made a corny joke one day that it would be humid in the office. Oh well, they stayed with me anyway and we formed an efficient and friendly team of translators.

Since our family still lived on the farm, I commuted every day the ninety kilometres between the farm and Ottawa, and back in the evening. It was a gruelling pace, but Elaine and I had now made up our minds to move back to Ottawa sometime within the year, and so the commuting was only temporary.

I soon found out that I could not have been more fortunate in my choice of associates. They were both very charming young ladies as well as excellent translators. Ginette Dulac was French Canadian from the Beauce region of Quebec, and Marianne Marin was from France.

Together, they brought with them language skills that could satisfy the linguistic peculiarities of Canadian as well as European French, should the need arise.

The project took about a year to complete and ended in the latter part of 1984. I looked for other government translation contracts to bid on, but had trouble finding any. There had been a federal election a few months before with a Conservative government under Brian Mulroney replacing the short-lived Liberal government of John Turner. With the change in government came a change in policy with respect to contracting out government work. Contracting out was severely cut back. Government contracts became as scarce as hens' teeth.

I was sorry that I had to let my two excellent associates go. We had worked very well together and had become more than just associates; we had become friends. Fortunately, they were both able to find good jobs with the federal government as translators.

Meanwhile, our family jumped off another of Ray Bradbury's cliffs. We had made the decision to move to Ottawa, and the time we had planned for the move had come. It was August 1984, and the school year would soon start. We didn't want to put our girls through the turmoil of having to change schools in mid-session, so we went ahead with our plan to move. Elaine and I spent some time in Ottawa looking for an appropriate home for our family. We eventually found exactly what we were looking for in the part of Ottawa called The Glebe. Here is the cliff we had jumped off: we were moving to Ottawa and a new home with monthly mortgage payments staring us in the face, and neither of us had a job or even a contract. We could last for a little while with no money coming in, but the contract scene was not good and neither was the job market for a couple of middle-aged candidates who had been out of that market for ten years. I quickly started building some wings.

In the late seventies, while still at Bell Canada, I had been seconded by Bell to the Canadian International Development Agency (CIDA) to do some preliminary engineering for microwave telecommunication systems, first in the Congo, which was known as Zaire at the time, and later in Rwanda. I decided to approach CIDA to enquire if there were any technical translation contracts in the cards for the telecommunications field. I sought out the engineer in charge of the telecommunications sector, Colin Billowes, since he was known to me because of my previous work with CIDA.

As soon as Colin set eyes on me, he blurted out, "Where the hell have you been? We've been trying to find you for a couple of months. Jacques, our senior telecommunications specialist is leaving and we haven't been able to fill the job. We want to offer you the job." It was with great pleasure, and some relief, that I accepted and started my new career on the tenth of December, 1984.

The next eighteen years in my CIDA job took me to the far corners of the Earth, helping developing countries build modern telecommunications systems that could respond to the modern needs of those countries. Developing countries have many needs that must be satisfied, not the least of which are in the fields of health, food, education, potable water, and several others. As well as attacking these humanitarian needs, it is also essential that developing countries build modern infrastructure, which is necessary to create sound economies and viable business sectors. The telecommunications sector is one of those essential infrastructures without which economies and business cannot thrive in today's modern world.

As mentioned earlier, in 1995 Elaine and I decided to end our relationship. Our views on things in general and our philosophies were diverging. Daughter Amanda graduated from Concordia University in Montreal in June 2007 with a degree in languages and now works as a translator in Ottawa. Jessica also lives close by in Ottawa with Peter and our lovely granddaughter, Cara.

In 2002, I retired after travelling the world for a fascinating eighteen years with CIDA. My retirement years have brought with them a treasure — a treasure of time that I can now devote to my present love: writing. I wrote my first book, which was on the Canadian Arctic, in 1994 while still working with CIDA. Since my retirement in September 2002, I have written two more books on the Arctic, stimulated by my experience in the north while with Bell Canada in the sixties and seventies. The present book is my fourth.

When we sold the farm in 1984 to move back to Ottawa, we did not sell the three hundred acres surrounding Lake of the Old Uncles. The cabin is still there, little the worse for the wear, and is still my oasis of quietude and meditation in a surrounding world of chaos. It is a wonderful place to create and develop writing ideas and themes to be further developed and written up on my computer in the city. I find that I can no longer write without a computer, but neither can I bring a computer to the cabin to do the physical act of writing there. Somehow, the cabin and the computer are a contradiction of terms that I have yet to resolve in my mind. They seem to be in two different worlds, and yet I need them both to write. I still haven't completely understood this wrinkle.

Part Seven

THE BEST OF FRIENDS

IN 1963, MY WORK HAD taken me from Montreal to live in Quebec City. In the ensuing year, a co-worker suggested that I meet his brother-in-law, Douglas Dacres, because he felt Doug and I shared common interests when it came to nature. How right he was. We hit it off right from the beginning and have maintained a warm friendship from that time until the present, even though we live some five hundred kilometres apart. A major area of common interest that we discovered was being outdoors in nature and all that that entails.

We found that we were natural canoeing partners — Doug paddled on the right, and I on the left, so we were always on our preferred sides. But we both suffer from a not-unusual disability — I more than he. Under panic situations, it seems that we confuse left for right and vice-versa. It is the bowman's job to be on the lookout for submerged, but dangerously shallow, rocks, and to immediately inform the steersman to take evasive action as well as take evasive action himself. Every split second counts, especially in a rapid. Screaming "turn right, RIGHT!" when one means "turn left" can be less than appropriate, as a large dent in our aluminum canoe soon testified. How to solve this problem? The solution was simple, once we thought of it. We bought two rolls of adhesive tape, one green the other black. We really wanted green and red for starboard and port, but couldn't find red. Black would have to do. In the bow, we taped a foot-long length of green along the flat top of the right gunwale, in plain view of the bow paddler. On the left, a length of black. Toward the stern we did the same thing for the rear paddler. Now we yelled, "Turn black" or "turn green." Our system has never failed us.

We cut our teeth paddling the Metabetchouan River north of Quebec City in the late sixties, naming points of interest, and at times frustration, as we went along. "Underwear Rapids" got its name because I ran it alone in minimal attire in case I flipped — which I didn't. The origin of "Bear Crap Portage" is pretty obvious. "Blueberry Campsite" came about because the fruit was so abundant there that we could lie in our floorless tent at night and reach a hand outside to grab some to nibble on. One evening, as darkness was falling, a series of three, very short portages separated by only a few dozen metres became "The Miserables" and the campsite following them became "Miserable Campsite" because we were so wet and tired with unpacking, carrying over slippery leg-breaking boulders, and repacking that we just couldn't seem to get a fire started. We went to bed completely worn out and cold with just a hunk of cheese in our stomachs, thankfully falling into a deep, restoring sleep. "Don't line 'em Rapids" came from the experience of trying to line them, and finding out in the middle that we were blocked by sheer rock plunging into the river. We ended up bushwhacking our gear and canoe up a long and steep forested hill to be able to get around the rest of the fast water. "Burnt Bacon Campsite" commemorates the site of a less than successful breakfast. The howling we heard at "Wolf Point" made it all worthwhile.

When snow covered the ground we went winter camping, generally without a tent. We built lean-tos for shelter. We had never done this before, but we learned fast. Winter is not too forgiving. We learned to sleep with our beer, eggs, and boots in our sleeping bags. Boots? Yes, especially boots. Leather boots absorb moisture during the day, from the snow on the outside and from sweat on the inside. Let them freeze overnight and you can't get into them in the morning. We learned not to thrash around too much at night out of consideration for the eggs.

Doug came up with a brilliant idea for the cooking and night fire. In the winter, a fire tends to gradually sink down through the snow into a pit several feet down. Not a good situation. One day Doug brought along a large, rectangular cookie tin for a winter expedition, and he had told me to bring one, too. We cut down two eight-foot spruce saplings about three to three and a half inches in diameter and laid them on the snow, parallel and as far apart as the shorter dimension of the rectangular tins. We then nailed our two cookie tins end-to-end, lengthwise along the middle section of the fir poles, providing a flat 1' x 4' surface to build a fire on. A hole in the snow soon formed beneath the cookie tins, but the fire did not sink into the snow because the two long spruce poles were supported on the surface of the snow at both ends. And if we found that the fire was a bit too far away from the shelter, we picked the whole contraption up like a stretcher and moved it closer. It was a portable fire and worked like a charm.

In the spring, Doug and I would get up at four o'clock in the morning to see and listen to the arriving birds along the shore of the St. Lawrence River. We botanized in the forest to discover new flowers, trees, and mushrooms. We fished together, canoe-camping along wild rivers and lakes; as long as it was outdoors in the wilderness, we were happy as larks, and we are still at it.

We still get together two or three times a year for some such outdoor activity or other, despite our five-hundred kilometre separation.

In 1980, the year I finished the cabin, Doug and I instituted a yearly spring ritual. In the month of May, we spend two, three, and sometimes four days at the cabin. We bring up food and drink — steaks, spaghetti, beans and wieners, eggs and bacon, and all the other good things that go into breakfasts, lunches, and suppers, plus a few beers, sometimes a bottle of wine. We spend our days rambling the woods, eating, discovering new facets of nature — there are always new ones. There are mountains to be climbed to high rocky lookouts with vistas to the dim, misty horizons of other, far away mountains. In the evening, there are important subjects to discuss, dissect, and explore, books to read, stars, planets, and the moon to be enjoyed, alternated at times with the soothing sound of rain falling gently on the roof of our warm, dry cabin. And there are hours to be spent in the deep, restoring sleep of the physically tired and satisfied.

Doug and I are now on the wrong side of seventy-five and we are not without realizing that there will be that big deadline to meet some day in the not too distant future. We can speak frankly about it and without fear. It is a part of nature. A couple of years ago, we made an agreement. When one of us finally leaves this beautiful earth, the survivor will speak at his service, and recite Robert Service's poem, "Good-Bye, Little Cabin."

The little cabin on the shores of Lake of the Old Uncles has meant so much to both of us.

O dear little cabin, I've loved you so long,
And now I must bid you good-bye!
I've filled you with laughter, I've thrilled you with song
And sometimes I've wished I could cry.
Your walls they have witnessed a weariful fight,
And rung to a won Waterloo:
But oh, in my triumph I'm weary tonight —
Good-bye, little cabin, to you!
    Your roof is bewhiskered, your floor is a-slant,
Your walls seem to sag and to swing;
I'm trying to find just your faults, but I can't —
You poor, tired, heart-broken old thing!
I've seen when you've been the best friend that I had
Your light like a gem on the snow;
You're sort of a part of me — Gee! but I'm sad;
I hate, little cabin, to go.
    Below your cracked windows red raspberries climb;
A hornet's nest hangs from a beam;
Your rafters are scribbled with adage and rhyme,
And dimmed with tobacco and dream.
"Each day has its laugh," and "Don't worry, just work."
Such mottoes reproachfully shine.
Old calendars dangle — what memories lurk
About you dear cabin of mine.
    I hear the world-call and the clang of the fight;
I hear the hoarse cry of my kind;
Yet well do I know, as I quit you tonight,
It's Youth that I'm leaving behind.
And often I'll think of you, empty and black,
Moose antlers nailed over your door:
Oh, if I should perish my ghost will come back
To dwell in you, cabin, once more!
    How cold, still and lonely, how weary you seem!
A last wistful look and I'll go.
Oh, will you remember the lad with his dream!

The lad that you comforted so.
The shadows enfold you, it's drawing to-night;
The evening star needles the sky:
And huh! But it's stinging and stabbing my sight —
God bless you old cabin, good-bye!
Robert Service: *Collected Poems of Robert Service*

It seems to be a long trip since starting out life in my grandparents' country inn in St-Rémi D'Amherst in July of 1931. As a writer, I know all about deadlines and I have met many. As I mentioned earlier, I have accepted the fact that I have a big one to meet not too many years down the line. I am certainly not looking forward to meeting it, but when I have to, I want to end my trip through this world in a small, peaceful field surrounded by forest and crystal-clear lakes, just outside St-Rémi — a field where lie my grandparents Isaïe and Amanda, my parents Nason and Jeanne, my only sibling Jacques, who died in infancy, cousins, uncles, aunts, and friends. I will lie just a kilometre or so from Hôtel Thomas, where I was born so long ago.

The circle will be complete. Come to think of it, it won't really have been such a long trip after all, will it? Only a kilometre or so from Hôtel Thomas to the cemetery, but Oh! the moments I will have had, and the marvels I have seen in that kilometre.

Meanwhile, I must go. There are other lakes and rivers to dip a paddle in, other forest paths to tread, other cliffs to jump off, other loves to discover, other words to write — and, of course, there will be the comforting welcome of the cabin whenever I crave its healing caress.

Marquis Book Printing Inc.

Québec, Canada
2008